WHY ME?

When Bad Things Happen to Good People

EDWARD D. ANDREWS

WHY ME?

When Bad Things Happen to Good People

Edward D. Andrews

Christian Publishing House
Cambridge, Ohio

Copyright © 2018 Edward D. Andrews

All rights reserved. Except for brief quotations in articles, other publications, book reviews, and blogs, no part of this book may be reproduced in any manner without prior written permission from the publishers. For information, write, support@christianpublishers.org

Unless otherwise stated, Scripture quotations are from Updated American Standard Version (UASV) Copyright © 2022 by Christian Publishing House

WHY ME? When Bad Things Happen to Good People by Edward D. Andrews

ISBN-10 : 1945757957

ISBN-13 : 978-1945757952

Table of Contents

Book Description 8

Preface.. 9

Introduction 11

CHAPTER 1: Is God Responsible for the Bad Things that Happen to Us? 13

    The Sovereignty of God and the Problem of Evil.................... 13

    Understanding God's Indirect and Direct Responsibilities...... 15

    The Role of Free Will in Suffering 18

    Navigating the Theodicy Debate: Is God Just?......................... 21

CHAPTER 2: How Can We Cope When Tragedy Strikes? 25

    Understanding the Grieving Process Through the Lens of Faith 25

    Biblical Figures Who Endured Hardship 28

    Trusting God's Wisdom and Timing 31

    Prayer and Community Support as Coping Mechanisms........ 33

CHAPTER 3: Why Is Life So Unfair?................................. 37

    Biblical Insights into Life's Difficulties..................................... 37

    The Consequences of Sin in the World 39

    The Perils of Comparing Our Lives with Others 42

    The Value of Trials in Spiritual Growth 44

CHAPTER 4: Does God Step in and Solve Every Problem if We Are Faithful?... 48

    Unraveling the Prosperity Gospel 48

    Faithfulness vs. Prosperity: A Biblical Perspective 50

    The Role of Prayer in Problem-Solving.................................... 53

    Knowing When and How God Intervenes............................... 56

CHAPTER 5: Do Not Let Doubts Destroy Our Faith....... 59

    The Nature of Doubt in the Christian Experience 59

    Biblical Examples of Doubters Turned Believers 61

    Strategies for Overcoming Doubt through Scripture 64

    The Role of Christian Community in Battling Doubt 67

CHAPTER 6: Your Feelings Don't Have to Control You (Prayer as Rational Self-Talk) 70

    Emotional Intelligence from a Christian Perspective 70

    Identifying Destructive Emotional Patterns 73

    Scriptural Teachings on Emotional Management 76

    The Role of Prayer in Emotional Wellness 79

CHAPTER 7: The Power of Forgiveness in Overcoming Pain 83

    Biblical Principles of Forgiveness 83

    The Psychological and Spiritual Benefits of Forgiving 86

    Overcoming the Barriers to Forgiveness 89

    The Role of Repentance and Restitution 92

CHAPTER 8: The Problem of Suffering in the Old Testament 96

    The Story of Job: An Examination 96

    Israel's Suffering and Jehovah's Plan 99

    Lessons from the Psalms: The Language of Lament 101

CHAPTER 9: What the New Testament Teaches About Suffering 104

    Suffering as a Christian Virtue 104

    Pauline Perspectives on Suffering 107

    The Ultimate Suffering: The Crucifixion of Christ 109

CHAPTER 10: Finding Purpose in Pain 112

    Understanding the Refining Nature of Suffering 112

    God's Ultimate Plan for Our Lives 114

    Transforming Pain into Ministry 117

CHAPTER 11: The Role of the Church in Alleviating Suffering 120

    The Biblical Mandate for Community Support 120

    How the Early Church Responded to Suffering 122

    Modern-Day Applications for Churches 125

CHAPTER 12: Understanding Hell: Eternal Torment or Eternal Destruction? 129

    Scriptural Insights into the Nature of Hell 129

    Debunking Common Misconceptions 131

    The Role of Judgment and Mercy 133

CHAPTER 13: Coping Mechanisms: Healthy vs. Unhealthy 136

    Scriptural Guidance on Coping Strategies 136

    Identifying and Avoiding Unbiblical Coping Mechanisms .. 138

    Turning to Scripture and Prayer for Comfort 141

CHAPTER 14: The Hope of Resurrection and Eternal Life 144

    The Christian Belief in the Resurrection of the Dead 144

    The Assurance of a New Heaven and New Earth 146

    Living in the 'Now' with Eternal Perspectives 149

CHAPTER 15: Conclusion: Where Do We Go from Here? 153

    Drawing Near to God in Times of Suffering 153

    Building Resilience through Faith and Community 156

    Preparing for Future Trials: Equipping Ourselves Spiritually 158

APPENDIX Other Related Books by Edward D. Andrews 162

Edward D. Andrews

Book Description

Why do bad things happen to good people? This question has troubled humanity for generations, yet it seems to weigh particularly heavy on the hearts of believers. 'WHY ME?: When Bad Things Happen to Good People' delves into this timeless dilemma, offering biblical wisdom and compassionate insights for those wrestling with life's most challenging questions.

Drawing from a conservative Christian perspective grounded in a literal interpretation of the Scriptures, this book offers a comprehensive guide on the age-old problem of evil and suffering. 'WHY ME?' explores the nature of God's sovereignty, the reality of human free will, and the role these elements play in the trials we face. Through biblical exegesis and practical counseling advice, this book aims to assist Christians in navigating the emotional, spiritual, and psychological complexities of suffering.

Chapters are carefully designed to address various facets of the issue, from understanding God's role in adversity to finding healthy coping mechanisms through faith and community. Whether you're struggling with personal grief or a church leader seeking to support those suffering, 'WHY ME?' offers a well-rounded, Scripturally-grounded perspective that balances spiritual sensitivity with psychological understanding.

Embark on this transformative journey towards spiritual resilience and discover how faith can light the way even in the darkest moments.

Preface

As you hold this book in your hands, it's likely you've found yourself asking a question that has been contemplated by theologians, philosophers, and ordinary people for centuries: Why do bad things happen to good people? Perhaps you're grappling with a recent tragedy, struggling to make sense of the chaos that has turned your life upside down. Maybe you're a spiritual leader, seeking answers to offer solace to those in your care who are hurting. Regardless of the reason, you're here because you seek understanding—both theological and practical.

It's important to state upfront that this book doesn't claim to offer a one-size-fits-all solution to the problem of suffering. Instead, it aims to be a comprehensive guide, weaving together Scriptural exegesis, insights from Christian theology, and practical counseling advice to address the diverse aspects of suffering. It is written from a conservative Christian viewpoint, deeply rooted in a literal interpretation of the Scriptures, and adheres to the objective Historical-Grammatical method of interpretation.

The chapters in this book have been crafted to cover a broad spectrum of topics related to suffering. Starting with an exploration of God's sovereignty and the challenges posed by the existence of evil, we will progress into more nuanced topics like emotional management, coping mechanisms, and the role of the Christian community in offering support. While each chapter can be read as a standalone essay, the book as a whole aims to offer a cohesive understanding of suffering from a Christian perspective.

Moreover, as we dive into these complex issues, it's crucial to keep an open heart and mind. There are some questions for which we may not find easy answers. In some instances, we may need to embrace the mystery and paradox inherent in Christian teachings. Yet, even in the absence of complete understanding, this book aims to provide you with the tools to confront suffering with resilience, wisdom, and above all, faith.

I pray that as you journey through these pages, you find not only the intellectual answers you seek but also the spiritual comfort that comes from drawing near to God. May you emerge with a fortified faith, better equipped to face life's trials and to offer guidance to others who are navigating the treacherous waters of suffering.

Edward D. Andrews

Author of over 220 books

Introduction

In the landscape of human experience, few phenomena perplex and unnerve us as much as suffering. From natural disasters to personal tragedies, from lingering illnesses to sudden loss—each form of suffering presents its own unique set of questions that begs for answers. This book exists because you, like many before you, seek clarity amid the cloudiness of adversity. While the Preface shed light on the methodology and theological grounding of this work, let us now delve into the framework and purpose that will guide our exploration.

The first part of this book delves into the foundational theological aspects that come into play when bad things happen to good people. It is a thorough investigation into the character of God—His sovereignty, His justice, and His role in the world's suffering. We will analyze Scriptural accounts and interpretations to understand God's indirect and direct responsibilities in the realm of human suffering. Why? Because a right view of God is pivotal to making sense of suffering.

From there, we move to a psychological and emotional angle, examining how humans react when confronted with the inexplicable. We'll probe into the Biblical guidance on coping with emotional turmoil and how to find equilibrium amid disequilibrium. At this juncture, we'll also dissect common misunderstandings about coping mechanisms—differentiating between what is Biblically endorsed and what isn't.

Then we turn our attention to the ecclesiastical support systems in place for dealing with suffering. What role does the Church have? How can a Christian community rally to offer true solace and meaningful support to its hurting members? This part of the book also explores how suffering has been historically understood and addressed within the Christian community, offering lessons we can glean for today.

Finally, the book closes by exploring the forward path. How do we live in a world marred by suffering? How do we continue to find joy, meaning, and purpose? And most importantly, how can suffering transform us into better believers, better neighbors, and better humans?

The subject matter we're about to explore isn't easy. In fact, it's likely to hit close to home for many. But if you are searching for an approach that neither shies away from the hard questions nor offers platitudes as answers, then you're in the right place. May this book serve as a reliable guide as you grapple with the complexities of suffering from a grounded, Scripturally faithful standpoint.

Let the exploration begin.

CHAPTER 1: Is God Responsible for the Bad Things that Happen to Us?

The Sovereignty of God and the Problem of Evil

When tragedy strikes or when life seems overwhelmingly unfair, one question often resounds in the hearts of believers: Is God responsible for the bad things that happen to us? This chapter aims to provide a balanced, Scriptural answer to this intricate question. The essence of our inquiry centers around two pivotal concepts: the sovereignty of God and the problem of evil.

The Sovereignty of God: Defined

Before delving into the complexities of suffering, it's crucial to establish what is meant by God's sovereignty. In simplest terms, the sovereignty of God refers to God's supreme authority and control over His creation. Nothing happens without His knowledge or outside of His realm of authority. As Paul wrote to the Romans, "For from him and through him and to him are all things. To him be glory forever. Amen" (Romans 11:36, ESV).

The Problem of Evil: A Cosmic Dilemma

The problem of evil has been one of the most enduring challenges to theism. In theological circles, the question often arises as to how a good, omniscient, and omnipotent God could allow evil and suffering in the world He created. The existence of evil is often cited as incongruent with the character of an all-loving, all-powerful God.

The Object Lesson of Human Suffering

However, understanding God's role in suffering requires acknowledging that He didn't design suffering but allows it as an object lesson. God permits suffering to demonstrate the consequences of human independence from His sovereignty. The existence of evil and suffering serves as an experiential lesson for humanity, elucidating the inherent limitations of human autonomy and the necessity of divine governance. It's crucial to note that suffering isn't a tool God employs to build character, endurance, or growth. Instead, it serves as a vivid illustration of the fallout that ensues when humanity chooses to act apart from divine guidance and wisdom.

Simple Foreknowledge: A Clarification

Here, it's essential to introduce the concept of Simple Foreknowledge, which helps us appreciate the relationship between God's foreknowledge and human freedom. According to this perspective, God knows the future but doesn't causally determine it. His foreknowledge is more like the foreshadowing of events to come, rather than a deterministic force. If events were to happen differently, God's foreknowledge would also be different. Thus, God's foreknowledge doesn't rob us of our free will or culpability. Instead, it serves as an "infallible barometer," merely reflecting the choices that free moral agents will make.

Divine Justice and Human Responsibility

Given God's sovereignty and foreknowledge, how then do we reconcile the existence of evil and suffering? We must accept that God's allowance of suffering is neither arbitrary nor malevolent but serves a divine purpose. Moreover, we must not overlook human responsibility. While God may allow suffering as an object lesson, the direct causality of many tragedies lies squarely on human sinfulness or negligence.

God's Response to Suffering

Lastly, it's vital to acknowledge that while God allows suffering, He is not indifferent to it. Scripture is replete with instances where God offers comfort, guidance, and provision amid adversity. He may not intervene to prevent every tragedy, but He is a constant presence, providing the means for spiritual and emotional healing.

In summary, God's sovereignty doesn't make Him the author of suffering and evil; instead, He allows these realities as a stark object lesson for humanity. His foreknowledge doesn't dictate our choices but reflects them, thereby preserving human responsibility. And while God's allowance of suffering can be difficult to comprehend, we can rest assured that He provides the resources for us to cope, survive, and even thrive amid adversity.

As we proceed through this book, we'll delve deeper into the emotional, psychological, and spiritual aspects of this complex issue. But the foundation remains clear: God's sovereignty and human freedom co-exist in a divine tapestry, whose ultimate design is beyond human understanding but within the scope of divine wisdom and love.

By grappling with these complexities, we take a crucial step toward reconciling our faith with the harsh realities of life, deepening our understanding of God's character, and fortifying our spiritual resilience for the challenges that lie ahead.

Understanding God's Indirect and Direct Responsibilities

The question "Is God responsible for the bad things that happen to us?" confronts us when life takes unexpected, often tragic turns. Such inquiries often expose the tension between our understanding of God's character and the reality of human suffering. In this chapter, we will explore the notions of God's indirect and direct responsibilities to better appreciate the dynamics at play when bad things happen to good people.

Delineating God's Sovereignty

The sovereignty of God serves as the bedrock upon which our understanding rests. Sovereignty implies that God maintains ultimate control and authority over His creation. The Scriptures repeatedly affirm this, stating, for example, "In him we live and move and have our being" (Acts 17:28, ESV).

Understanding Indirect Responsibility

When we talk about God's indirect responsibility, we are exploring the idea that God allows a world where suffering can occur, though He doesn't willfully inflict this suffering upon us. The root cause of most suffering traces back to human actions or to the broader consequences of living in a fallen world. God permits these circumstances to persist because they serve as object lessons. Such lessons are harsh reminders of what happens when human beings act independently of God's will or when they diverge from His original design for creation.

God's Direct Responsibility: A Rarer Category

Instances where we might conceive of God as directly responsible for events in our lives are considerably less frequent. These are moments where God intervenes in human history in a visible, manifest way. Take, for example, the parting of the Red Sea or the plagues upon Egypt. These were divine acts meant to achieve specific ends, and while they might involve suffering or hardship, their purpose was to fulfill God's righteous plan.

Human Freedom and God's Foreknowledge

Understanding the concept of Simple Foreknowledge can help us reconcile the seeming contradiction between human freedom and God's omniscient nature. God's foreknowledge, in this view, is like an infallible barometer, reflecting rather than constraining future events. The choices of free moral agents will manifest regardless of what God knows beforehand, but His foreknowledge enables Him to prepare, plan, and ultimately work His will, even through human actions.

Suffering as an Object Lesson

God allows suffering, not to cultivate personal growth or character development, but as an object lesson. This lesson underscores the limitations and consequences of human independence from His sovereignty. Suffering serves as a form of experiential education, revealing to mankind their need for God's governance. It illustrates the outcome when humanity tries to walk apart from Him, and it drives home the indispensable quality of God's sovereignty.

The Purpose in Permissiveness

Why would a loving God allow such lessons? The answer lies in the ultimate purpose of these object lessons: to steer humanity back towards recognizing God's sovereignty and the futility of human independence. While this may be a painful method, the aim is redemptive. It serves as a constant reminder that independence from God results in suffering, motivating individuals to seek alignment with His will.

God's Provisions Amid Suffering

Although God allows suffering, He is far from indifferent to human plight. He provides spiritual resources and means of grace to help believers navigate the complexities of life's difficulties. Passages like Romans 8:28 ("And we know that for those who love God all things work together for good") remind us that, in His sovereignty, God can turn even the bitterest experiences into opportunities for deepening our relationship with Him.

Judging God's Responsibility

As we evaluate God's direct or indirect responsibility, we need to acknowledge that our human perspective is limited. Our judgments about God are often constrained by our finite understanding and temporal constraints. We look at a single thread and make assumptions about the entire tapestry that God is weaving throughout history.

To sum up, God's responsibility for the bad things that happen to us is more nuanced than a cursory glance might suggest. He has both indirect and direct roles in the unfolding events of our lives, but these are always governed by His character, which is unchangingly good, just, and loving. God allows suffering, not as a divine form of punishment or as a means to foster human growth, but as an object lesson designed to highlight the perils of human autonomy apart from His will.

Understanding this complex interplay between God's sovereignty, human freedom, and the existence of suffering can equip us with a more robust theology. This theological framework, in turn, can serve as an invaluable resource as we navigate the real-world experiences of hardship and loss, ensuring that our faith remains steadfast in the God who is, ultimately, the author of all things, and whose plans for us are for welfare and not for evil (Jeremiah 29:11).

The Role of Free Will in Suffering

The relationship between human suffering and God's role in it is a complex and multifaceted issue, particularly when considering the influence of free will. In this chapter, we explore the question: "Is God responsible for the bad things that happen to us?" through the lens of human freedom and its impact on suffering.

Defining the Framework: God's Sovereignty and Human Free Will

A proper understanding of God's sovereignty and human free will serves as the essential backdrop for this exploration. Sovereignty speaks to God's ultimate authority and control over His creation. While God is sovereign, He has also granted human beings free will—the capability to make decisions independent of divine intervention.

God's Sovereignty and Simple Foreknowledge

Before delving into the role of free will, let's consider God's foreknowledge. Under the view of Simple Foreknowledge, God possesses complete awareness of all future events, including those contingent on human decisions. Importantly, this foreknowledge doesn't causally determine events. God knows what will happen because it will happen, not the other way around. This notion ensures that human freedom remains intact, rendering God's foreknowledge like an infallible barometer—it doesn't control the weather, but it perfectly reflects it.

Free Will as the Catalyst for Suffering

Human free will can act as a catalyst for much of the suffering we experience. Consider the countless number of bad things that happen due to human choices—crime, wars, and acts of cruelty, to name a few. These events originate from human will and actions, far removed from God's design for His creation.

God's Indirect Responsibility

In a world laden with free will, God permits suffering to happen. He doesn't cause it but allows it, often as an object lesson highlighting the problems stemming from human independence from His sovereignty. The act of permitting suffering is an indirect responsibility on God's part. It serves as a powerful testimony to the inherent flaw in human beings choosing to walk their path away from God's guidance.

The Conundrum of Natural Disasters and Illnesses

But what about natural disasters or illnesses, which don't directly stem from human choices? Even in these situations, we could argue that they are still a result of the fallen state of the world, a consequence of collective human rebellion against God's sovereignty. These occurrences remind us of the brokenness that exists when the world is not aligned with God's divine will.

Free Will and Moral Evil

Furthermore, the existence of moral evil—wrongdoing that arises from human choices—testifies to the reality of free will. God allows us to choose between good and evil, and it's that very choice that gives rise to moral evil when people opt against God's law. God does not cause this suffering but permits it as an object lesson.

The Importance of Freedom for Genuine Love

Why does God permit free will, knowing it leads to so much suffering? One reason might be that freedom is a necessary component for genuine love and relationship. Without free will, humanity couldn't freely choose to love God or one another. Obligatory love is not love at all; it's mere compliance.

Redemptive Possibilities and Suffering

While God didn't design suffering to cultivate personal growth, His sovereignty allows Him to bring redemptive outcomes out of even the worst situations. This doesn't make the suffering good but shows that God can manifest good outcomes from bad situations, although this isn't the purpose of suffering.

Limitations of Human Understanding

Our attempts to understand the complex interaction between God's sovereignty, free will, and suffering are ultimately limited by our human perspectives. We only have a partial view, unable to see how all the pieces fit into God's greater plan.

The question of God's responsibility for suffering must account for the intricate interplay between His sovereignty and human free will. God's foreknowledge, unfettered by the constraints of causality, shows He is aware of our choices and their outcomes, but it doesn't predetermine them. Free will stands as a monumental factor in the occurrence of suffering, largely as a result of human autonomy from God's sovereignty.

God's indirect responsibility for suffering, therefore, arises from His permissive will. He allows it to happen as an object lesson for humanity, not as a means to foster growth, endurance, or character. This lesson is severe, but it's crucial for humanity to understand the consequences of divorcing itself from God's sovereignty. While our free will often leads us into suffering, it also offers us the choice to return to God, acknowledge His sovereignty, and find a peace that surpasses all understanding (Philippians 4:7).

Navigating the Theodicy Debate: Is God Just?

Theodicy is the theological endeavor to reconcile the existence of an omnipotent, benevolent God with the prevalence of evil and suffering in the world. This question is not new; it has been a point of discussion and contemplation for millennia. In this chapter, we'll navigate the theodicy debate, examining whether God is just in the face of human suffering.

The Complexity of Theodicy

The problem of evil has been a point of deep reflection and varying answers within Christian thought. Solutions have ranged from Augustinian theodicies, which view evil as a privation of good, to Irenaean theodicies that see suffering as a means for soul-making. However, for our discussion, we maintain that God does not cause suffering to foster growth, endurance, or character but allows it as an object lesson.

Simple Foreknowledge and Human Freedom

As we discuss theodicy, it's important to clarify the nature of God's foreknowledge. According to the Simple Foreknowledge view,

God knows everything that will happen but does not determine these events. This perspective allows for genuine human freedom while preserving God's omniscience. God's foreknowledge does not interfere with or predetermine human actions.

Human Freedom and Suffering

Many instances of suffering are a direct result of human choices. When we exercise our free will in ways contrary to God's will—when we lie, steal, cheat, or cause harm—we often bring about suffering. God's allowance for free will essentially means that He permits us to face the natural consequences of our actions as an object lesson.

God's Justice in Permitting Suffering

From a theological standpoint, the allowance of suffering is not indicative of a lack of justice on God's part. God is entirely just, but His justice doesn't negate the existence of free will or the resultant suffering. Rather, His justice is displayed in how He judges human actions, rewarding good and punishing evil (Romans 2:6-8).

Cosmic Justice

Although earthly justice is not always served, God's cosmic justice ensures that all accounts will be settled, whether in this life or the next. The concept of cosmic justice assures us that no act of suffering or evil will go unnoticed or unaddressed by God.

The Fall and Its Consequences

The doctrine of the Fall in Genesis accounts for the moral and natural evil in the world. When Adam and Eve chose to disobey God, their rebellion led to a world tainted by sin and its repercussions, including suffering. While God did not cause this suffering, He permitted it to serve as an object lesson about the consequences of human autonomy from His sovereignty.

The Justice of God in Redemption

God's justice is also manifest in the plan of redemption through Jesus Christ. Despite the human propensity for causing suffering and evil, God provides a way for reconciliation and restoration. This provision demonstrates His justice by offering forgiveness through the sacrifice of Jesus, provided we repent and believe (Acts 17:30-31).

Is Suffering Always a Consequence of Sin?

While suffering often results from human sin, it's critical to remember that not all suffering is a direct consequence of individual wrongdoings. Jesus Himself clarified this in the case of the man born blind, stating that the man's condition was not due to his or his parents' sin (John 9:1-3).

The Implications of Denying God's Justice

Rejecting the idea of God's justice in light of suffering could lead us down a slippery slope. If God is not just, the entire foundation of Christian theology crumbles. The promise of redemption, eternal life, and divine justice all become meaningless.

Suffering in Eschatological Perspective

Lastly, it is essential to consider suffering within the broader eschatological framework. The Bible assures us of a time when God will wipe away all tears, and there will be no more suffering (Revelation 21:4). This future reality does not negate the pain of the present but provides a hopeful context within which to understand it.

Navigating the theodicy debate requires a nuanced understanding of God's character, human free will, and the nature of suffering. While the issue is complex, the Christian narrative offers a coherent framework within which to understand it. God's justice is not compromised by the existence of suffering. Rather, God allows suffering to serve as an object lesson about the dire consequences of human independence from His sovereignty. In this light, God remains just, and His justice will be fully realized in His time.

CHAPTER 2: How Can We Cope When Tragedy Strikes?

Understanding the Grieving Process Through the Lens of Faith

When tragedy strikes, we find ourselves plunged into a complex maze of emotions, questions, and existential dilemmas. As we confront these challenges, it's crucial to approach them through a faith-based perspective, acknowledging the broader context in which suffering occurs and the eternal hope that provides solace and understanding.

Acknowledging Grief: The First Step

Firstly, it's essential to acknowledge the reality of your grief. Grief is a natural human response to loss, and it's something the Bible doesn't shy away from discussing. David grieved for his child (2 Samuel 12:16-23), Jesus wept for Lazarus (John 11:35), and the Apostle Paul acknowledged sorrow (2 Corinthians 2:4). Therefore, your grief isn't a sign of weak faith but a reflection of your humanity.

What Scripture Teaches About Grief

Various passages in the Scriptures provide insight into dealing with grief. The Book of Job, for instance, is an extended meditation on suffering and grief. Here, God does not dismiss Job's sorrow but allows him space to express it. Paul's letters also exhort believers to "mourn with those who mourn" (Romans 12:15). Through Scripture, we find that God doesn't condemn grief but walks alongside us in it.

The Object Lesson of Suffering

It's crucial to approach grief with the understanding that God has allowed suffering to serve as an object lesson about the consequences of human autonomy from His sovereignty. Tragedies are not punishments from God, nor are they designed to develop our character or endurance. Rather, they are the result of living in a fallen world. Understanding this is essential for framing our grief and seeking comfort.

The Compatibility of God's Foreknowledge and Human Freedom

When coping with tragedy, some may wonder, "Did God know this would happen?" According to the Simple Foreknowledge view, God knows everything that will occur, but His knowledge doesn't determine these events. This perspective helps us understand that while God knew the tragedy would happen, He did not cause it. This knowledge allows us the comfort of knowing that our freedom and God's foreknowledge are compatible. The tragedy happened not because God willed it, but because we live in a world where suffering exists.

The Role of Prayer

Prayer is an indispensable resource for anyone navigating grief. Through prayer, we are invited to cast all our anxieties onto God, knowing that He cares for us (1 Peter 5:7). It is in these moments of vulnerability that we often feel God's comfort most profoundly. While prayer doesn't offer a quick fix, it provides a pathway for dialogue with God, who is the "Father of mercies and God of all comfort" (2 Corinthians 1:3).

The Community of Faith: A Pillar of Support

The community of faith plays an essential role in helping us through the grieving process. Whether it's through the ministry of presence, acts of kindness, or the sharing of Scriptural truths, other believers can provide invaluable support. Remember that the Bible admonishes us to bear one another's burdens (Galatians 6:2).

Long-term Coping: The Importance of Resilience and Faith

As time passes, the intensity of grief may lessen, but the need for resilience and faith remains. Resilience doesn't mean forgetting or entirely overcoming the pain; rather, it means learning to live in a 'new normal.' Here, faith acts as a support structure, grounded in the promises of God and the hope of a world without suffering and pain (Revelation 21:4).

The Eschatological Hope: A Future Without Suffering

Understanding grief through the lens of faith allows us to maintain an eternal perspective. While suffering is a present reality, Scripture teaches that it is not an everlasting one for those in Christ. There will come a day when God will wipe away all tears, and there will be no more suffering (Revelation 21:4).

Moving Forward: Action Steps

As we navigate grief, it's helpful to lean on spiritual disciplines such as prayer, Bible study, and fellowship. We should also consider seeking professional help when needed, as mental health is as critical as spiritual well-being.

Coping with tragedy is an intricate process, made even more complicated by the myriad of emotions and existential questions that arise. Nonetheless, by understanding that God allows suffering for broader, often incomprehensible, reasons and by leaning on the resources of faith, we can find a form of solace and hope that transcends our current circumstances. It's in this assurance that we find the strength to live through grief, holding onto the promises of God and the eternal hope that offers ultimate restoration and healing.

Biblical Figures Who Endured Hardship

Tragedies and difficulties are as old as human history, and they leave no one untouched. Throughout the pages of Scripture, we see a gallery of individuals who faced harsh circumstances. Learning from these biblical figures can help us navigate our own hardships, all while understanding that God allows suffering as an object lesson about the limitations of human autonomy from His sovereignty.

Job: The Quintessence of Suffering

The story of Job stands as a monumental narrative on the experience of suffering. Job, who was blameless and upright, lost his wealth, his health, and his children in quick succession. Yet, Job teaches us the virtue of patience and the necessity of clinging to God, even when things make little sense. Job came to realize that God's ways are beyond human comprehension, and it is not our place to question His wisdom.

Joseph: Overcoming Betrayal

Joseph's life was marked by extreme ups and downs. Sold into slavery by his own brothers, falsely accused and imprisoned, Joseph's story is one of unceasing hardship. However, the thread running through Joseph's life is his steadfast faith in God. He never compromised his integrity and eventually saw God's providence in his life, revealing that suffering often has larger, unfathomable purposes that are aligned with God's foreknowledge.

David: A Man After God's Own Heart

David, a man "after God's own heart," was far from immune to trials. His life was fraught with persecution, family betrayal, and personal failure. The Psalms are full of his raw emotions, giving voice to his despair, hope, and steadfast faith. Through it all, David learned to rely not on his understanding but on the sovereignty of God.

Paul: Suffering for the Gospel

The Apostle Paul faced beatings, imprisonment, and ultimately execution for the sake of Christ. Despite these difficulties, Paul counted them as nothing compared to the glory to be revealed (Romans 8:18). His letters are a testimony to the enduring hope he had in Christ, emphasizing that our earthly troubles are momentary in light of eternal life.

Jesus: The Suffering Servant

Above all, we look to Jesus, the "suffering servant," who endured the ultimate form of suffering by taking on human sin and dying on the cross. He was "a man of sorrows and acquainted with grief" (Isaiah 53:3). His example shows us that the greatest act of love came through the greatest form of suffering.

Coping Mechanisms from Biblical Figures

1. **Surrender to God's Will**: Job's ultimate submission to God's sovereignty was his key to enduring his trials.
2. **Maintain Integrity**: Joseph's refusal to compromise his moral principles served him well in the end.
3. **Emotional Transparency**: David's candidness in his prayers can guide us in channeling our grief and sorrow constructively.
4. **Perspective Shift**: Paul's eternal perspective can help us look beyond our immediate circumstances.
5. **Unwavering Faith**: The enduring faith that Jesus exhibited in His earthly ministry serves as the ultimate example for us.

Simple Foreknowledge and Enduring Hardships

Understanding that God's foreknowledge does not causally determine human choices is important for coping with suffering. Just because God knows an event will occur does not mean He wills it to happen in a malicious sense. This understanding preserves the integrity of human free will and the notion of a benevolent God, while also respecting God's omniscience.

Practical Applications

1. **Prayer and Meditation**: Regular prayer can provide emotional release and bring divine wisdom into your difficult circumstances.

2. **Scripture Study**: Regularly studying the Scriptures will fortify your spirit and give you practical advice on enduring hardships.

3. **Community Support**: Don't underestimate the power of a supportive faith community. Surround yourself with people who can offer spiritual counsel and emotional support.

4. **Seek Professional Help**: While spiritual solutions are crucial, consulting professionals for mental and emotional health is also important.

Though the Bible features individuals who encountered various forms of suffering, each story is a testament to enduring faith and reliance on God's sovereignty. When you find yourself in the valleys of life, remember that God allows suffering to teach humanity an object lesson about the consequences of human independence from His perfect will. Through the lives of these biblical figures, we can find inspiration and practical tips for coping with our own hardships. By looking to them and applying the lessons they offer, we can navigate through our trials with the resilience and faith they exemplified.

Trusting God's Wisdom and Timing

As human beings, we are inherently limited by our finite understanding and time-bound perspective. However, God, in His infinite wisdom and omniscience, operates on a plane far beyond human comprehension. Learning to trust God's wisdom and timing can be one of the most liberating and comforting strategies to cope with the tragedies and trials that life inevitably brings. This chapter will explore the essence of trusting God's wisdom and timing, drawing from biblical examples and practical applications.

Trusting God's Wisdom

In Scripture, God's wisdom is consistently demonstrated as incomparable and unsearchable. As the Apostle Paul notes in Romans 11:33, "Oh, the depth of the riches and wisdom and knowledge of God! How unsearchable are his judgments and how inscrutable his ways!"

1. **Job's Experience**: One of the most poignant examples is Job, who was confronted with unimaginable suffering. Job questioned God's wisdom but ultimately had to acknowledge God's unsearchable understanding (Job 42:1-6).

2. **Solomon's Prayer**: Solomon specifically prayed for wisdom to govern God's people, acknowledging that human wisdom is insufficient for life's complexities (1 Kings 3:9).

Trusting God's Timing

Understanding that God's timing is perfect, even when it doesn't align with our plans, is crucial for spiritual peace.

1. **Abraham and Sarah**: They had to wait for many years before God fulfilled His promise of giving them a child. Despite the long wait, God's timing was perfect (Genesis 21:2).

2. **Jesus' Ministry**: Even Jesus operated under God's perfect timing. He started His ministry at a specific age and told His

disciples that His hour had "not yet come" on several occasions (John 7:6).

Practical Applications of Trusting God's Wisdom and Timing

1. **Daily Surrender**: Start your day by surrendering your plans to God. Acknowledge His greater wisdom and perfect timing.
2. **Scriptural Meditation**: Ground yourself in Scriptural truths about God's wisdom and timing, such as Ecclesiastes 3:1-11 and James 1:5.
3. **Accountability**: Share your struggles with a trusted spiritual mentor or a friend who can provide biblical advice and prayer support.
4. **Stay Engaged**: While waiting for God's timing, continue to engage in good works and spiritual disciplines.
5. **Spiritual Discernment**: As you grow in your relationship with God, ask Him for discernment to understand His will better, while acknowledging that His ways are higher than ours (Isaiah 55:8-9).

Simple Foreknowledge: Understanding God's Role

It is essential to recognize that God's foreknowledge is not a determinant of human actions or events. Rather, His foreknowledge is a kind of infallible "barometer" of the future. He knows what will happen because it will happen, not the other way around. In this, we see that human free will is preserved, along with the integrity of God's omniscience. Understanding this aspect can free us from fatalistic views that can inadvertently make God responsible for human suffering.

Trust in Prayer

Pour out your heart in prayer, even when circumstances make it challenging to trust God. Remember that God hears the prayers of the righteous (James 5:16) and cares about your suffering.

Counseling and Community Support

While it's crucial to trust God, He has also provided us with community and professionals who can help us navigate through suffering. It's biblical and wise to seek counseling and fellowship during difficult times.

Trusting God's wisdom and timing does not mean adopting a passive approach to life's challenges or absolving ourselves of responsibility. It means acknowledging that God's ways are infinitely wiser and His timing more perfect than anything we could devise. Even as God allows suffering to teach humanity an object lesson, a life lived in sync with God's wisdom and timing will better equip us to navigate the tragedies and complexities of our existence. Therefore, as we continue to face life's trials, let us endeavor to lean not on our own understanding but on the omniscient and timeless wisdom of God (Proverbs 3:5-6).

Prayer and Community Support as Coping Mechanisms

In times of tragedy and suffering, two potent mechanisms to cope are through prayer and community support. Both avenues are rooted deeply in Scripture and have been time-tested methods for sustaining individuals through the challenges that life brings.

The Importance of Prayer

Prayer is a crucial element in building and maintaining a relationship with God. At the core of prayer is the act of opening up our lives, concerns, and struggles to God. The Bible teaches that prayer has power; James 5:16 says, "Therefore, confess your sins to one another and pray for one another, that you may be healed. The prayer of a righteous person has great power as it is working."

1. **The Model of Jesus**: In the life of Jesus, we find a pattern of prayer in the face of various challenges, including impending suffering (Luke 22:42).
2. **Honesty in Prayer**: God values an open and honest heart. When we approach Him in prayer, it's essential to pour out our real emotions and struggles. David exemplified this in many of his psalms (Psalm 13).
3. **Intercession**: While praying for ourselves is important, Scripture also encourages us to intercede for others. Intercession magnifies the community aspect of the church and underscores the importance of collective spiritual well-being (1 Timothy 2:1-2).
4. **Trusting God's Sovereignty**: Even as we pray, it's crucial to remember that God allows suffering to reveal the flaws in human independence from His sovereignty. Understanding this, we can approach prayer with a willingness to yield to His perfect plan, even when it involves suffering.

Community Support: The Role of the Church

1. **The Early Church**: The practice of bearing one another's burdens can be traced back to the early church, where believers "had all things in common" (Acts 2:44-45).
2. **Accountability and Encouragement**: Having a trusted circle of believers can serve as a mechanism for spiritual accountability. They can also offer necessary spiritual encouragement and Scriptural insights (Hebrews 3:13).
3. **Spiritual Gifts for Edification**: God has endowed the church with various spiritual gifts for the edification of the body (1 Corinthians 12:7). In times of tragedy, these gifts can be particularly impactful for healing and comfort.

4. **Practical Support**: The church can be an instrumental source of practical aid in times of crisis, from financial assistance to emotional support.

Uniting Prayer and Community

1. **Prayer Groups and Meetings**: Establishing or joining prayer groups can provide collective spiritual power and offer emotional support.
2. **Pastoral Care**: Trained spiritual leaders can offer Biblical counsel that complements community support, often opening new perspectives on God's will and timing.
3. **Scriptural Foundation**: Both prayer and community are rooted in Scripture. By aligning our practices with biblical guidelines, we open the door for God's work in and through us.

The Aspect of Simple Foreknowledge

In dealing with tragedy, the understanding of God's foreknowledge as being like an "infallible barometer" allows us to preserve human freedom. Knowing that God's knowledge of the future doesn't constrain our actions can be liberating. This understanding means that God's perfect knowledge doesn't violate human freedom or become the cause of our suffering.

Practical Steps

1. **Be Intentional**: Don't hesitate to ask for prayer and support or offer them to others. It's what the body of Christ is for.
2. **Stay Rooted in Scripture**: Surround yourself with God's Word, perhaps focusing on passages that emphasize God's care and sovereignty.

3. **Engage in Corporate Worship**: Sometimes, collective worship can bring solace and perspective that individual reflection cannot.

4. **Seek Professional Christian Counseling**: Sometimes tragedies require professional support that is rooted in a biblical worldview.

When tragedy strikes, we are never alone. God, in His infinite wisdom, has provided us with the mechanisms of prayer and community support to cope with the harsh realities of life. While God allows suffering to teach humanity the folly of independence from His sovereignty, He doesn't abandon us in our suffering. Instead, He provides us with tools that are both spiritually enriching and emotionally comforting. Therefore, let us utilize these God-given resources as we navigate through the tragedies that are an inevitable part of our human experience.

CHAPTER 3: Why Is Life So Unfair?

Biblical Insights into Life's Difficulties

One of the most common questions people grapple with is the issue of life's inherent unfairness. Whether it's inexplicable suffering, unearned privileges, or unmerited pain, it's only natural to ask, "Why is life so unfair?" The Bible offers invaluable perspectives that help us understand and cope with this perplexing issue.

The Question of Fairness in the Bible

The issue of fairness is hardly new; it has been explored extensively in the Scriptures. Take, for example, the story of Job. He was a man of integrity and piety, yet he faced horrendous trials. Even some of the psalmists questioned the fairness of life, wondering why the wicked prosper while the righteous suffer (Psalm 73).

1. **Sin and Its Consequences**: The entry of sin into the world through Adam and Eve resulted in a broken system that often manifests as unfairness (Romans 5:12).

2. **Human Choices and Free Will**: Human beings, endowed with free will, make choices that contribute to the unfairness in the world (James 1:13-15).

3. **The Sovereignty of God**: As Christians, we believe that God is sovereign, yet He allows human suffering and unfairness to teach humanity the folly of independence from His rule.

Four Key Biblical Principles

1. **The Reality of a Fallen World**: The world we live in is fundamentally flawed due to sin. This reality necessitates an environment where unfairness thrives (Romans 8:20-22).
2. **The Justice of God**: God is just and fair, and He promises to set things right, whether in this life or the life to come (2 Thessalonians 1:6-9).
3. **The Grace and Mercy of God**: While life might seem unfair, it's also essential to remember that we've all benefited from God's unmerited grace (Ephesians 2:8-9).
4. **Human Responsibility**: As believers, we have an obligation to mitigate unfairness where we can, acting justly and loving mercy (Micah 6:8).

God's Foreknowledge and Human Suffering

The concept of Simple Foreknowledge suggests that while God knows the future, His knowledge doesn't cause the events to happen. In understanding life's unfairness, this preserves the essential freedom that humans possess. God foreknows our experiences of unfairness but does not cause them.

How to Cope with Life's Unfairness

1. **Cultivate a Robust Theology**: A well-grounded understanding of God's character can be a stronghold in times of questioning and doubt (1 Peter 5:10).
2. **Spiritual Disciplines**: Practices like prayer, fasting, and Bible study can provide comfort and clarity when grappling with life's inequities (James 4:8).
3. **Community and Accountability**: Surround yourself with a supportive Christian community that can provide encouragement and share burdens (Galatians 6:2).

4. **Action and Advocacy**: Be proactive in challenging the systems and structures that perpetuate unfairness. Act justly, love mercy, and walk humbly with your God (Micah 6:8).
5. **Seek Professional Christian Counseling**: In extreme cases, it might be beneficial to seek counsel from a qualified Christian professional who can provide biblical perspectives and coping mechanisms.

Life's inherent unfairness can be unsettling and challenging to our faith. However, the Bible offers a myriad of insights that not only help us understand this issue but also equip us to cope with it. As we navigate through the labyrinth of life's complexities, it's vital to anchor ourselves in the immutable character of God and the eternal truths of His Word.

Though God allows unfairness as a part of the human experience to underscore our need for His sovereignty, His overarching purpose is not to harm but to bring about an eventual and perfect justice. Therefore, while we may not understand all the intricacies of life's unfairness, we can rest in the assurance that our sovereign God is in control, working all things out for His glory and our good (Romans 8:28).

The Consequences of Sin in the World

The question of life's unfairness is one that perplexes many, both Christians and non-Christians alike. When faced with inexplicable pain, loss, or hardship, it's natural to question the nature and purpose of such suffering. In this chapter, we delve into the theological aspects that contribute to the seeming unfairness in the world, particularly focusing on the role of sin and its consequences.

The Genesis of Unfairness: The Fall

In the Garden of Eden, Adam and Eve enjoyed a perfect relationship with God, free from pain, suffering, and injustice.

However, their decision to disobey God introduced sin into the world (Genesis 3). Sin has profound implications for the fairness of life; it disoriented the moral compass and distorted the fabric of existence (Romans 5:12).

The Pervasiveness of Sin

The Apostle Paul teaches us that all have sinned and fall short of the glory of God (Romans 3:23). Sin is not limited to one group of people or to particularly egregious acts. It's a universal condition that affects every person and, by extension, the world we live in. Consequently, we witness a plethora of injustices and sufferings, from individual hardships to systemic issues like poverty and inequality.

The Sovereignty of God

The doctrine of God's sovereignty teaches us that Jehovah is in control of all things, even in the presence of human sinfulness and the suffering it engenders. God allows these conditions to persist to teach humanity an important lesson: that our autonomy is flawed and that we cannot navigate life without acknowledging His sovereignty.

The Consequences of Sin

1. **Physical Suffering**: Illness, decay, and ultimately death are direct consequences of sin in the world (Romans 6:23).
2. **Emotional Pain**: Anguish, grief, and mental suffering are often intertwined with sin, either our own or that of others affecting us.
3. **Social Consequences**: Discrimination, inequality, and other forms of social injustice can be traced back to the sinful nature of man.
4. **Spiritual Death**: Perhaps the most significant consequence is the separation from God that sin causes, necessitating a Savior (Isaiah 59:2).

God's Foreknowledge and Human Free Will

Understanding God's foreknowledge in the context of suffering and sin can be enlightening. God knows what will happen, but this knowledge doesn't determine our choices. He permits human beings to exercise their free will, even when it leads to unfairness or sin, without His foreknowledge interfering with human autonomy. Therefore, God's foreknowledge acts like an "infallible barometer," neither causing nor preventing the future but tracking it accurately.

Christian Responsibility

1. **Personal Repentance**: One of the first steps in addressing life's unfairness is acknowledging our own sinful nature and repenting (Acts 3:19).
2. **Social Action**: Christians should engage in rectifying injustices (James 1:27).
3. **Spiritual Guidance**: Walking in obedience to God's Word can mitigate the personal and collective consequences of sin (Psalm 119:11).
4. **Prayer and Dependence**: Continual prayer and reliance on God provide the spiritual strength to navigate through an unfair world (Philippians 4:6-7).
5. **Seek Counsel**: Sometimes, the burden of life's unfairness is too great to bear alone, and wise counsel should be sought (Proverbs 11:14).

The unfairness we see in the world is a direct consequence of sin. While God allows this unfairness, His purpose is not to torment humanity but to underscore our utter dependence on His sovereign rule. As Christians, our role is not passive; we are called to action, both in our personal lives and in society at large, in ameliorating the consequences of sin.

Understanding God's sovereign character and His foreknowledge can give us peace, even when we are confounded by life's complexities.

While God does not cause the unfairness or suffering we encounter, He allows them as an object lesson for humanity. It is through this lens that we can begin to navigate the unfair terrain of life, ever reliant on God's sovereignty and ever committed to doing His will.

The Perils of Comparing Our Lives with Others

The propensity to compare ourselves with others is an almost universal human tendency. At times, these comparisons can lead to feelings of inadequacy, jealousy, or even despair. In a world where social media often portrays an idealized version of reality, it becomes even more challenging to avoid comparing our lives to those of others. As we navigate through this issue, it's essential to ground our understanding in the teachings of Scripture and the wisdom it offers to find contentment and purpose.

The Age-Old Temptation to Compare

The act of comparison is not a modern phenomenon. It has deep roots in human history and even in the Bible. From Cain and Abel to the Prodigal Son's older brother, comparison has been a destructive force that corrodes relationships and stokes discontentment.

The False Promise of Comparison

Comparing ourselves with others often arises from a false belief that life is a zero-sum game; if someone else gains, we must lose. However, this mindset ignores the truth that each person's journey is divinely orchestrated by God, who allows events in our lives for reasons we may not fully understand, but are part of His larger lesson about the flaws in human independence from His sovereignty.

Theological Considerations: The Sovereignty of God

As believers, we affirm the sovereignty of God in all aspects of life. While unfairness and inequality may exist in the world, it's important to remember that God allows these conditions. God's sovereignty is not meant to induce suffering but to illustrate the limitations of human autonomy and the need for divine guidance.

The Pitfalls of Comparison

1. **Spiritual Myopia**: Comparing our lives with others can obscure our spiritual vision, making it difficult to see God's work in our lives.

2. **Covetousness and Envy**: Such comparison can lead to coveting what others have, which is explicitly warned against in the Ten Commandments (Exodus 20:17).

3. **Dependence on Earthly Standards**: Comparison usually leans on worldly standards of success, wealth, or attractiveness, rather than godly virtues like kindness, patience, or faithfulness.

4. **Diminished Self-Worth**: Constantly measuring ourselves against others can severely undermine our sense of self-worth.

5. **Impact on Relationships**: It can strain friendships and family bonds, sowing discord and creating divisions (James 3:16).

God's Foreknowledge and Comparison

Understanding God's foreknowledge can help us grapple with the impulse to compare ourselves with others. God's knowledge of future events doesn't restrict our free will or predetermine our actions. Knowing that God's foreknowledge is like an "infallible barometer" allows us to be free moral agents, making choices that align with His will or against it. Our decisions, in turn, are a reflection of our characters, not the result of divine determinism.

Finding Contentment in God

1. **Understanding Identity**: Realize that your worth is not based on comparison but on your creation in the image of God (Genesis 1:27).
2. **Godly Contentment**: Paul teaches us the secret of contentment in any and every circumstance (Philippians 4:11-13).
3. **Gratitude**: Gratefulness for what we have can disarm the temptation to compare (1 Thessalonians 5:18).
4. **Cultivating Virtues**: Focusing on developing Christian virtues can help shift attention away from external comparisons to internal growth.
5. **Prayer and Reflection**: In times of struggle, turning to prayer can provide comfort and a renewed focus on God's sovereignty (Philippians 4:6-7).

The inclination to compare ourselves to others is a perilous one, fraught with spiritual, emotional, and relational dangers. Although God allows the conditions that make such comparisons tempting, He does so as an object lesson to underscore our need for Him. As free moral agents, we have the responsibility to choose contentment and satisfaction in God over the false allure of comparison. By doing so, we honor God's sovereignty, affirm our identity in Him, and fortify our spiritual lives against the corrosive effects of envy and discontent.

The Value of Trials in Spiritual Growth

Navigating the labyrinth of life is no small feat. As humans, we often grapple with difficult questions surrounding fairness and equality. For the faithful, understanding the place of trials and tribulations in the broader context of spiritual growth is a crucial endeavor. This chapter aims to explore the value of trials in spiritual growth, mindful of the theological framework that God allows suffering to demonstrate the limitations of human independence from His sovereignty.

Human Conception of Fairness

Our initial understanding of fairness is generally based on reciprocity, merit, or equal distribution of goods and opportunities. However, a Biblical perspective offers a more complex understanding of justice and fairness, deeply rooted in the wisdom and providence of God.

The Theology of Trials

We must emphasize that God does not design suffering for the purpose of fostering growth, endurance, or character in a person. However, suffering exists and God permits it for a reason—to illustrate the limitations of human autonomy. It's an object lesson that teaches us about the importance of acknowledging the sovereignty of God.

Trials as Refining Fires

1. **Spiritual Insight:** Though not divinely orchestrated for personal growth, trials often function as refining fires that sharpen our spiritual discernment.
2. **Humility:** Hardships have a way of humbling us, making us acutely aware of our frailties and limitations.
3. **Godly Wisdom:** The book of James tells us that if we lack wisdom, we should ask God who gives generously (James 1:5). Often, the wisdom we seek is forged in the furnace of affliction.
4. **Strengthening Faith:** Trials can deepen our faith as we realize our dependence on God for sustenance and guidance (1 Peter 1:6-7).

God's Foreknowledge and Free Will

Understanding God's foreknowledge aids in putting trials in perspective. God's prior knowledge of future events doesn't constrain human freedom. He knows what will happen, but this foreknowledge doesn't make those events occur. This preserves our agency, allowing us to freely react to the trials that befall us.

The Problem of Comparing Trials

1. **Subjectivity**: The temptation to compare our trials to those of others is often rooted in subjective interpretations of 'severity,' which doesn't offer a fair evaluation.
2. **Unique Purpose**: Since each person's spiritual journey is distinct, comparing trials is counterproductive to understanding the lessons that may be gleaned from them.

Navigating Trials

1. **Seeking Guidance**: In times of hardship, turning to Scripture provides invaluable guidance (2 Timothy 3:16-17).
2. **Community Support**: The church community serves as a source of spiritual and emotional support (Galatians 6:2).
3. **Prayer**: Through prayer, we establish a direct line of communication with God, inviting His intervention and wisdom into our situations (Philippians 4:6-7).
4. **Self-Examination**: Trials often call for self-examination, prompting us to align our lives more closely with Scriptural principles.

Coping Mechanisms

1. **Grace**: Extending grace to ourselves and others is key to navigating the complexities of life's trials.

2. **Acceptance**: Acknowledging that trials are a part of the human experience helps in coping with them.
3. **Active Faith**: Putting faith into action through good works offers a constructive way to deal with trials (James 2:17).

Life's trials are enigmatic yet universal experiences. Though God does not engineer these difficulties to test or refine us, He permits them for a more profound lesson: to remind us of the insufficiency of human independence. Trials serve as object lessons, teaching us the value of surrendering to God's sovereignty. They prompt us to delve deeper into our spiritual reserves, to cling tighter to our faith, and to emerge with a fortified spirit. Even if God's foreknowledge knows the path we might take, it does not constrain us from freely responding to life's challenges. It serves as an infallible barometer of the future, giving us the assurance that even in the midst of trials, God's providence is ever-present.

CHAPTER 4: Does God Step in and Solve Every Problem if We Are Faithful?

Unraveling the Prosperity Gospel

One of the most misleading and prevalent ideas within some Christian circles is the so-called "Prosperity Gospel." This doctrine asserts that faithfulness to God equates to earthly prosperity, happiness, and the resolution of all life's problems. This chapter aims to provide a Scripturally-based dissection of the Prosperity Gospel and offers an alternative view grounded in sound theology and the objective Historical-Grammatical method of interpretation.

The Lure of the Prosperity Gospel

The Prosperity Gospel appeals to our innate desire for comfort and security. The promise of material abundance and problem-free living is tantalizing, but it profoundly misrepresents the nature and will of God. At the heart of this doctrine is a distorted view of God as a divine vending machine—insert faith, and out pops blessings.

The Biblical View of God's Providence

Scripture gives us a much richer and nuanced understanding of God's character and His relationship with humanity. God is not obligated to solve all of our problems even if we are faithful. He doesn't promise a life free of hardships; in fact, Jesus explicitly says, "In this world you will have trouble" (John 16:33).

Misinterpretations that Fuel Prosperity Teaching

1. **Faith as a Force:** Some proponents argue that faith is a sort of spiritual currency. This is a distortion of passages like Mark 11:24, ignoring the context and broader Scriptural teachings about the nature of faith and prayer.
2. **Giving to Get:** The misuse of passages like Luke 6:38 ("Give, and it will be given to you") suggests that our actions can obligate God to bless us materially. This fails to consider that God's blessings are not always of a material nature.
3. **Health and Wealth as Divine Rights:** Verses like 3 John 1:2 are cited to suggest that God wants us to be prosperous in a materialistic sense. Such interpretations lack sound exegetical support.

God's Permissive Will and the Value of Trials

While God does not design suffering to foster growth or character, He allows it for a different reason—to underline the inherent flaw of human independence from His sovereignty. Suffering serves as a reminder that we cannot manage life's complexities on our own. God's permissive will, allowing hardship and suffering, serves as an object lesson in this regard.

Debunking Prosperity Claims with Scripture

1. **Paul's Suffering:** Despite being a faithful servant, the Apostle Paul endured numerous hardships, even expressing his "thorn in the flesh" (2 Corinthians 12:7-9). His experience flies in the face of Prosperity Gospel claims.
2. **Job's Trial:** Job was upright and faithful, yet he experienced immense suffering. His story serves as a reminder that faithfulness is not an insurance policy against hardship.

3. **Christ's Crucifixion**: The Prosperity Gospel is entirely incompatible with the sufferings of Christ, who was without sin yet endured the ultimate sacrifice.

True Blessings: Spiritual Over Material

1. **Internal Transformation**: God's blessings often come in the form of wisdom, spiritual growth, and a closer relationship with Him.
2. **Eternal Perspective**: God's blessings should be viewed in light of eternity, not just our current circumstances. This viewpoint reframes our understanding of what is truly valuable.

The Prosperity Gospel's claim that faithfulness will result in a problem-free life stands in stark contrast to the teachings of the Bible. While God does bless His children, these blessings are not solely, or even primarily, material. Furthermore, God allows suffering, not as a mechanism to build character or endurance, but as an object lesson revealing the inherent limitations of human independence. Theology that aligns with the full counsel of Scripture acknowledges that God's ultimate aim is not to make our earthly lives comfortable, but to draw us into a deeper, more meaningful relationship with Him, centered on His sovereignty and grace. This relationship equips us to navigate the trials of life, not by promising their absence, but by offering us the wisdom and spiritual resources to face them.

Faithfulness vs. Prosperity: A Biblical Perspective

The notion that God intervenes to resolve all of our difficulties if we are loyal to Him has pervaded certain segments of Christian culture. This chapter will scrutinize this belief by contrasting the concept of faithfulness against prosperity, all under the lens of a Biblically-consistent worldview.

The Essence of Faithfulness

In Biblical terms, faithfulness is a steadfast commitment to God and His Word. It isn't a transactional exercise but a relational one. In 1 Corinthians 4:2, Paul asserts, "Moreover, it is required of stewards that they be found faithful." The emphasis here is on integrity and fidelity to God, rather than on reaping material or circumstantial benefits.

Prosperity: A Multifaceted Issue

Prosperity can manifest in various forms—financial, physical health, or even circumstantial ease. However, it is essential to differentiate between prosperity as a cultural value and prosperity as a Biblical promise.

Faithfulness and Prosperity in the Old Testament

It's vital to examine the Biblical narrative to see how faithfulness and prosperity are presented. In the Old Testament, the Israelites were promised material blessings for obedience (Deuteronomy 28:1-14). However, these promises were specific to the covenantal relationship between Jehovah and Israel and were conditional upon their obedience.

Faithfulness and Prosperity in the New Testament

The New Testament paints a nuanced picture. Jesus never guarantees freedom from suffering or trials; in fact, He promises the opposite (John 16:33). Paul, a paragon of faithfulness, experienced hardships, persecution, and eventually, martyrdom. The New Testament, therefore, does not support the notion that faithfulness inevitably leads to earthly prosperity.

The Prosperity Gospel Examined

The Prosperity Gospel preaches that God's favor is manifested through material blessings and life's comforts. It often misinterprets and misapplies Scriptures like Malachi 3:10 and Luke 6:38. While the Bible does mention that God rewards faithfulness, it's crucial to acknowledge that these rewards are not necessarily materialistic and can often be spiritual or eternal in nature.

Problems with the Prosperity Gospel

1. **Neglect of the Sovereignty of God**: The Prosperity Gospel makes God out to be a cosmic bellhop, which undermines His sovereignty. The Bible teaches that God allows suffering, not as a means for growth but as an object lesson highlighting the limitations of human independence.

2. **Faulty Exegesis**: Many of the Scriptures used to support Prosperity teaching are ripped out of context, negating the original meaning intended by the authors.

3. **Eclipses the Eternal**: The Prosperity Gospel's emphasis on the here and now often overshadows the eternal life that Scripture continually points us to.

The True Nature of Faithfulness and Its Rewards

1. **Spiritual Maturity**: One of the genuine rewards for faithfulness is growth in spiritual maturity (Ephesians 4:11-13).

2. **Assurance and Peace**: Faithfulness cultivates a deeper relationship with God, which results in the inner peace that surpasses all understanding (Philippians 4:7).

3. **Eternal Rewards**: The New Testament speaks of crowns and rewards in heaven for those who have been faithful (2 Timothy 4:8; 1 Peter 5:4).

The Complexity of God's Will

Understanding God's will involves recognizing His decreed will, permissive will, and prescriptive will. In the grand tapestry of life, these aspects of God's will interact in complex ways we cannot fully comprehend. What we do know is that God allows suffering, not as a method to build character, but as an object lesson to humanity, underlining our limitations and need for His governance.

While it's natural to desire prosperity, the Scriptures clearly do not support the idea that faithfulness is a guaranteed path to material blessing or an absence of problems. Instead, faithfulness is its own reward—deepening our relationship with God and aligning our will with His. God's ultimate goal is not our temporary comfort but our eternal well-being and His glory. Understanding this liberates us from the disillusionment that can come from misplaced expectations and positions us to experience the richness of a life truly dedicated to God.

The Role of Prayer in Problem-Solving

Many Christians struggle with the relationship between faithfulness, prayer, and problem-solving. There's a pervasive belief that prayer can serve as a "magic bullet" to eradicate all life's challenges, but this thinking runs contrary to Scripture and even misunderstands the nature and purpose of prayer. This chapter aims to unfold a Biblically sound perspective on the role of prayer in addressing life's difficulties.

The Nature of Prayer

Prayer is not merely a transactional interaction with God where requests are made and either granted or denied. It's fundamentally relational—a way to align our will with God's and grow closer to Him. In the model prayer Jesus taught His disciples, the emphasis is on God's will: "Your will be done, on earth as it is in heaven" (Matthew 6:10, ESV).

Misconceptions About Prayer and Problem-Solving

1. **The Vending Machine Fallacy**: This notion posits that God will automatically dispense solutions when we input the correct 'prayer code.' This simplistic approach trivializes God's wisdom and sovereignty.
2. **The Quid Pro Quo Error**: This is the belief that our good behavior and faithfulness will lead to God solving all our problems. But the Bible does not endorse such a merit-based relationship with God.

The Role of Suffering

While God did not design suffering for personal growth or character development, He does allow it. Suffering serves as an object lesson that underscores humanity's inherent flaws when operating independently from God's sovereignty. Understanding this helps demystify why prayers for problem-solving might not result in immediate relief or solutions.

God's Sovereignty and Simple Foreknowledge

God knows what will happen, but this foreknowledge doesn't constrain our free will or the natural unfolding of events. His omniscience serves as a perfect barometer, not a puppet master pulling strings. Thus, God's foreknowledge does not negate the meaningfulness of our prayers or the genuineness of our free moral agency.

Prayer in the Old Testament

People like Moses, David, and Daniel prayed fervently, yet their lives were not devoid of problems. They experienced both miraculous deliverances and significant suffering. Their examples show that while God hears and values prayer, He does not promise an absence of difficulties.

Prayer in the New Testament

In the New Testament, prayer is often associated with a deepening of faith and a focus on the Kingdom of God. Paul encourages Christians to pray in all circumstances but tempers this by reminding them of the peace of God, not necessarily the removal of the problem (Philippians 4:6-7).

Biblical Principles on Prayer and Problem-Solving

1. **Prayer Aligns Us with God's Will**: Jesus' prayer in Gethsemane exemplifies this. He prayed for the cup to pass from Him but concluded with, "Nevertheless, not as I will, but as you will" (Matthew 26:39, ESV).

2. **Prayer Strengthens Us**: Even if the external circumstances don't change, prayer equips us with the spiritual fortitude to endure (Ephesians 6:18).

3. **Prayer Is Not a Formula**: There is no guaranteed "3-step process" to get what we want. God looks at the heart, not just the words (1 Samuel 16:7).

4. **God's Wisdom Surpasses Ours**: Sometimes what we perceive as a problem is part of a greater plan we cannot yet understand (Isaiah 55:8-9).

The Limitations of Prayer as Problem-Solving

1. **The Sovereignty of God**: God has the prerogative to say yes, no, or wait in response to our petitions.

2. **Human Free Will**: God allows individuals their agency, which sometimes results in painful consequences both for them and for others.

3. **The Inherent Flaw of Humanity**: As part of the ongoing object lesson, problems may persist to show us our inadequacies apart from God.

The purpose of prayer is not to manipulate God into solving all our problems but to deepen our relationship with Him and align our will with His. While God does not promise a problem-free life, He assures us of His ongoing presence and the ultimate triumph of His will. As we navigate life's complexities, may we approach prayer not as a quick fix but as a profound act of faith, trust, and surrender to the One who is sovereign over all.

Knowing When and How God Intervenes

One of the most perplexing questions believers face is when and how God intervenes in human affairs. Does our faithfulness precipitate His involvement? How can we discern God's action or inaction in our lives? While complete understanding evades us because of the divine mystery surrounding God's sovereignty, we can glean some principles from Scripture to guide us.

Faithfulness and Divine Intervention: Are They Connected?

There's a common misconception that God's intervention is proportionate to our faithfulness. However, Scripture doesn't endorse this cause-and-effect relationship. The Apostle Paul, whose faithfulness was exemplary, dealt with a "thorn in the flesh" despite his prayers for relief (2 Corinthians 12:7-9). Faithfulness to God does not guarantee a problem-free life, but it does promise the sufficiency of God's grace.

Understanding God's Sovereignty

God's sovereignty doesn't exist to serve human ends; rather, human events unfold under God's overarching governance. Even when suffering or hardship occurs, God's sovereignty remains intact. However, God doesn't design suffering to foster personal growth or character development. Instead, such trials serve as an object lesson, teaching us the inherent flaw in our independence from God's sovereignty.

God's Intervention in the Old Testament

In the Old Testament, Jehovah's intervention was evident in miraculous deliverances like the parting of the Red Sea and the fall of Jericho. However, His intervention was not solely a function of Israel's faithfulness. Sometimes God acted to fulfill His purposes or promises, irrespective of human merit (Genesis 50:20).

God's Intervention in the New Testament

Jesus' healings and miracles displayed God's compassion and power, yet they were also selective. Not everyone in Israel during His time was healed or delivered. In the New Testament writings, Paul and other Apostles faced considerable suffering despite their fervent prayers and faithfulness. God's interventions served higher divine purposes, often far removed from human understanding (Romans 8:28).

Signs of Divine Intervention

1. **Miraculous Events**: Sometimes God intervenes in ways that defy natural explanation, but these are the exceptions, not the rule.
2. **Alignment with Scriptural Principles**: Any perceived intervention should be weighed against the revealed Word of God. If an event contradicts Scriptural principles, its attribution to God would be suspect.
3. **The Witness of the Spirit**: While there's no indwelling of the Holy Spirit, the Spirit-inspired Word can give discernment about God's activities (Hebrews 4:12).
4. **Testimony of Fellow Believers**: Sometimes God's actions become more apparent through the collective insight and experiences of the community of faith (Matthew 18:20).

When God Doesn't Intervene: Factors to Consider

1. **The Sovereignty of God**: God reserves the right to act or not act based on His sovereign will.
2. **The Object Lesson of Humanity**: Some difficulties persist as part of the larger object lesson that humanity needs to learn about its flawed independence from God.
3. **God's Eternal Perspective**: What may seem as non-intervention to us might be part of a grander eternal scheme that we cannot yet comprehend.

How to Respond When God Seems Silent

1. **Continue in Faithfulness**: Just as Job remained faithful in his suffering, so should we continue in faithfulness regardless of divine intervention or the lack thereof (Job 1:21).
2. **Search the Scriptures**: Times of seeming divine silence are opportunities to delve deeper into God's Word for comfort and guidance (Psalm 119:105).
3. **Engage in Community**: The church body can offer support, wisdom, and communal prayer during such times (Hebrews 10:24-25).
4. **Reevaluate Expectations**: Sometimes the problem lies in our expectations of what God "should" do, rather than in God's actual promises.

The notion that God steps in to solve every problem if we are faithful is inconsistent with both the Old and New Testament accounts. God's intervention, or the lack thereof, serves His sovereign purposes, which often serve as an object lesson for humanity. While our faithfulness is a response to God's love and grace, it is not a currency to purchase divine intervention. As we navigate the complexities of life, it's crucial to lean not on our own understanding but to trust in God's sovereign wisdom and perfect will (Proverbs 3:5-6). Thus, whether or not we witness divine intervention, our call remains the same: to live faithfully and obediently in response to the God who is sovereign over all.

CHAPTER 5: Do Not Let Doubts Destroy Our Faith

The Nature of Doubt in the Christian Experience

In a life of faith, doubt is not an uncommon visitor. Christians, both new and seasoned, may at times grapple with questions and uncertainties that shake the foundations of their belief. The key is not to let these doubts consume and destroy our faith. By examining the nature of doubt within the context of the Christian experience, we can better understand how to address it constructively.

The Nature of Doubt

Doubt is not merely the absence of faith but is often a fluctuating state of mind that questions the validity or reliability of what is believed. It manifests in various forms: intellectual doubts about the truth of Scripture, emotional doubts triggered by life's hardships, and volitional doubts that question the cost of discipleship.

Biblical Examples of Doubt

The Bible is candid about individuals who experienced doubt. Thomas, aptly nicknamed "Doubting Thomas," needed physical proof of Jesus' resurrection (John 20:24-29). Even John the Baptist, from his prison cell, sent messengers to Jesus to clarify if He was indeed the Messiah (Matthew 11:2-3). Their doubts did not make them lesser Christians; rather, their experiences illustrate that doubt is not incompatible with genuine faith.

Sources of Doubt

1. **Intellectual Challenges**: Skepticism from scientific, historical, or philosophical angles can instigate doubt.

2. **Life's Trials**: When faced with suffering or injustice, one may question the goodness or even the existence of God. Here it's important to remember that suffering itself has not been engineered by God but is permitted to highlight humanity's flawed independence from His sovereignty.

3. **Social Influences**: Sometimes, doubt can stem from social circles that deride or challenge faith.

4. **Spiritual Warfare**: The Bible warns that Satan seeks to sow discord and doubt among believers (1 Peter 5:8).

Addressing Doubt

1. **Engage with the Word**: Scripture should be the go-to resource. A thorough understanding of God's Word can clarify misconceptions and reinforce faith (Psalm 119:11).

2. **Seek Wise Counsel**: Consult mature believers or church leaders. A supportive Christian community can offer insights and encouragement (Proverbs 11:14).

3. **Prayer**: While doubts may sometimes make prayer difficult, it remains a vital avenue for seeking clarity and solace from God (Philippians 4:6-7).

4. **Examine the Heart**: Sometimes, doubt is not an intellectual or theological issue but a matter of the heart. Sin or disobedience can be a barrier to faith (James 1:6-7).

5. **Understanding God's Character**: Recognizing the immutable nature of God's goodness, sovereignty, and wisdom can provide a stabilizing anchor for shaky faith (Hebrews 13:8).

Doubt vs. Unbelief

It's crucial to differentiate between doubt and unbelief. Doubt questions and seeks answers; unbelief is a settled disposition against belief. Doubt can lead to strengthened faith through the resolution of questions, while unbelief leads away from faith.

The Role of Doubt in Spiritual Maturity

While doubt is not a desirable state, navigating through it can result in spiritual maturation. Confronting and resolving doubts often leads to a deepened, more nuanced understanding of God and His Word. However, it's important to acknowledge that trials and doubts serve as object lessons, teaching us the inherent flaw in our independence from God's sovereignty.

Doubt is an almost inevitable part of the Christian journey, but it need not be its terminus. When channeled correctly, doubt can serve as a stepping stone rather than a stumbling block, deepening our understanding and appreciation of God's sovereignty and wisdom. Therefore, instead of fearing or avoiding doubts, confront them head-on through prayer, study, and godly counsel. The objective is not to rid ourselves of all questions but to bring those questions before God and His Word, letting them illuminate rather than obscure the path of faith.

Biblical Examples of Doubters Turned Believers

Doubt is an experience common to human beings, and Christians are no exception. While doubt can be unsettling, it is essential to remember that it is not the antithesis of faith but often an element within the journey of faith. The Bible contains vivid stories of individuals who grappled with doubt and emerged with a strengthened faith. These stories serve as both encouragement and guidance for Christians today.

1. Thomas: The Doubter Who Touched Faith

Thomas, often labeled as "Doubting Thomas," serves as a prime example of how doubt can be transformed into faith. When Jesus appeared to His disciples after His resurrection, Thomas was not present. Despite the other disciples' accounts, Thomas insisted he would only believe if he could touch Jesus' wounds (John 20:24-25). Eventually, Jesus accommodated Thomas' doubt and allowed him to touch His wounds, leading Thomas to a profound declaration of faith, "My Lord and my God!" (John 20:28).

2. John the Baptist: Questioning the Messiah in the Midst of Trials

John the Baptist is another notable figure who experienced doubt. After baptizing Jesus and witnessing the heavens open and the Spirit descend like a dove, John still found himself questioning Jesus' messiahship while languishing in prison. He sent his disciples to Jesus, asking, "Are you the one who is to come, or shall we look for another?" (Matthew 11:3). Jesus reassured him, citing the fulfilled prophecies (Matthew 11:4-6). His experience serves as an object lesson that sometimes our circumstances can cloud our spiritual vision, but it doesn't mean God has changed or failed.

3. Peter: From Denial to Proclamation

Peter, who once bravely declared that he would die for Jesus, ended up denying Him three times (Matthew 26:69-75). Despite his deep regret and doubt in himself, Peter was restored by Jesus (John 21:15-19) and went on to become a bold apostle, spreading the gospel far and wide.

4. Sarah: Laughter Turned to Joy

Sarah, the wife of Abraham, laughed when she heard that she would have a son in her old age (Genesis 18:12). Her doubt was not just in the biological impossibility but perhaps also in the audacious hope that God's long-awaited promise would be fulfilled. Yet, when Isaac was born, her doubt was turned into joy and faith (Genesis 21:6-7).

5. The Israelites: A Journey from Doubt to Dependence

The Israelites consistently doubted Jehovah's ability to provide for them and lead them to the Promised Land. Despite seeing miraculous provision like manna from heaven and water from a rock, they frequently grumbled against God and Moses. This doubt cost the first generation their entry into the Promised Land but also served as an object lesson for the next generation about the importance of faith and dependence on God's sovereignty.

6. Gideon: A Warrior Born Out of Doubt

Gideon's story shows that God can transform even the least likely candidates into His faithful servants. Gideon doubted when the angel of the Lord called him a "mighty man of valor" (Judges 6:12). Yet, through a series of events that confirmed God's power, Gideon's doubt was turned into daring faith.

Lessons for Today's Christians

1. **Temporary Doubt is Not Terminal**: Doubts do not mark the end of faith. Often, they are the uncomfortable avenues through which we deepen our understanding of God's nature and His promises.
2. **The Importance of Honest Dialogue with God**: These biblical figures didn't hide their doubts but took them directly to God or His representatives.
3. **Sovereignty and Suffering**: In suffering and doubt, we come to better understand the object lesson God has allowed: our utter dependence on His sovereignty.

4. **Community Support**: Surrounding yourself with a community of believers can be instrumental in overcoming periods of doubt. Faith is both personal and communal.

These biblical accounts reveal that doubt is not an unpardonable sin but a common experience on the path of spiritual growth. By examining how doubt was transformed into faith in the lives of these individuals, we find hope and practical guidance for our own faith journeys. The key takeaway is not to let doubt fester but to confront it with the objective truths of Scripture, thereby recognizing our need for God's sovereignty and guidance in all circumstances.

Strategies for Overcoming Doubt through Scripture

The Christian walk is not immune to the experience of doubt. Whether these uncertainties pertain to the nature of God, the reliability of the Scriptures, or even one's personal salvation, they can be deeply unsettling. However, it is critical to differentiate between destructive doubt and constructive doubt—the former paralyzes faith, while the latter can deepen it. Here, we'll explore various strategies to help you navigate through periods of doubt using the Scriptures as your guiding light.

1. The Power of Prayer and Scriptural Meditation

Doubt often occurs when we lose sight of God's character. Engaging in prayer and meditating on Scriptures can remind us of who God is. David often used this strategy in the Psalms. In Psalm 42:11, he asks, "Why are you cast down, O my soul?" but answers by putting his hope in God. Prayer helps us to align our will with God's, and Scripture meditation brings clarity to our minds.

2. Seek Verses That Address Your Specific Doubts

Scripture is abundant in answers if we seek them. Are you doubting God's love? Meditate on Romans 8:38-39. Concerned about your worth? Matthew 6:26 reminds us of how God values us. The key is to locate Scriptures that directly speak into your area of doubt and spend time reflecting on them.

3. Contextual Understanding of the Bible

Misinterpretation can breed doubt. To fully grasp a text, we should understand its context, original language, and its place in the larger narrative. Employing the historical-grammatical method of interpretation helps in achieving a clearer understanding of the Scriptures.

4. Memorization and Recitation

The ancient practice of Scripture memorization can be incredibly grounding. When doubt creeps in, reciting memorized verses can instantly bring peace and clarity. As Paul writes in Philippians 4:8, we are to think about things that are true, noble, and right. Memorizing Scripture aids in focusing our thoughts on these virtues.

5. Confess and Share with Trusted Believers

James 5:16 advises believers to confess their sins to each other and pray for each other. While doubt is not a sin per se, the principle of opening up to trusted friends or mentors for spiritual guidance and prayers can be very beneficial.

6. Resist the Urge to Lean on Human Understanding

Proverbs 3:5-6 warns us not to lean on our understanding but to acknowledge God in all our ways. Human logic is limited and fallible. During times of doubt, it's important to resort to divine wisdom through Scripture rather than relying solely on human reasoning.

7. Recognizing God's Sovereignty in Suffering

It's common to experience doubt in times of suffering. Remember Job, who had everything stripped away from him but never ceased in his integrity or faith in God's sovereignty. While it's difficult to understand why God allows suffering, we know from the Scriptures that it serves as an object lesson, highlighting our dependency on God's sovereignty rather than our own abilities.

8. Avoid Selective Reading and Interpretation

It's easy to pick verses that comfort us and avoid those that challenge us. However, this can lead to a skewed understanding of God's character and promises. A balanced reading of Scripture is essential for a well-rounded faith that can withstand doubt.

9. Engage with Apologetic Resources

While it's crucial to focus on the Scripture, reading apologetics can also help reinforce your faith. Authors who defend the faith can offer additional perspectives and arguments that you might not have considered, further fortifying your belief system.

10. Daily Surrender to God's Will

Sometimes doubt persists no matter how much we study or pray. In such moments, what remains is a simple, yet profound act of the will to surrender to God. Even if our heart and mind waver, a daily act of submitting to God's will can sustain us.

Dealing with doubt is a challenge that nearly all Christians face at some point. However, the Scriptures provide us with numerous resources to combat these unsettling periods in our faith journey. By integrating these strategies into our daily lives, we not only prepare ourselves to face future doubts but also deepen our existing faith. The ultimate aim is to realize our dependence on God's sovereignty, as it is through this acknowledgment that we find our way back from doubt to a resilient and fortified faith.

The Role of Christian Community in Battling Doubt

The Christian experience is not one that is meant to be lived in isolation. The Scriptures emphasize the importance of community in nurturing and sustaining our faith. Even more crucially, the Christian community serves as a bulwark against doubt, providing resources and relationships that can reinforce belief and challenge skepticism. This chapter explores the invaluable role that community plays in combating doubt.

1. Biblical Mandate for Community

Scripture is clear about the importance of community among believers. Hebrews 10:25 advises us not to forsake the gathering of believers, and in Acts 2:42-47, we see an idyllic picture of what Christian community can look like—devoted to teachings, to fellowship, to breaking of bread, and to prayers.

2. Emotional Support

One of the first lines of defense against doubt is emotional support from other believers. Emotional struggles often precede intellectual doubts, and a loving community can provide the emotional stability needed to fight off creeping skepticism.

3. Iron Sharpens Iron

Proverbs 27:17 says, "Iron sharpens iron, and one man sharpens another." In a similar vein, when believers come together, their collective wisdom and experiences serve to sharpen each other's understanding and convictions. Discussions and debates within a community can clarify misunderstandings and resolve questions, thus neutralizing doubt.

4. Accountability Partners

Being held accountable for one's actions and beliefs by someone else can be extremely helpful in periods of doubt. James 5:16 instructs us to confess our sins to one another and pray for one another. Though doubt is not a sin per se, accountability to another person can keep it from spiraling into destructive patterns.

5. Collective Worship

Worship is not merely an individual experience but a corporate one as well. Singing hymns, praying together, and participating in the sacraments within a community can create an atmosphere that dispels doubt. The collective affirmation of God's character serves as a reminder of truths we might forget when isolated.

6. Pastoral Guidance

Pastors and spiritual leaders in a community have usually undergone extensive theological training and can offer Biblically sound guidance. Their insights can provide answers to doctrinal questions that may be the source of doubt.

7. Testimonies of Faith

Hearing others share their own journeys, including their battles with doubt, can serve as powerful affirmations of the validity and resilience of Christian faith. Revelation 12:11 speaks of overcoming by the "word of their testimony." These testimonies can act as living proof that doubt can be conquered.

8. Service Opportunities

Engaging in service projects and mission work can sometimes offer the most powerful rebuttal to doubt. When we see God working through us to bless others, it's hard to question His existence or His goodness.

9. Reality of Suffering in the Community

In a Christian community, you are likely to encounter others who are also going through suffering, or have gone through it. Observing how they have navigated these experiences while maintaining their faith in God's sovereignty can offer powerful object lessons. This helps to remind us that suffering is not a sign of God's absence but rather serves to illustrate our need for Him.

10. Intellectual Resources within the Community

Within a well-rounded Christian community, there are usually individuals who have specialized knowledge in theology, apologetics, and philosophy. These individuals can offer valuable insights that can challenge and ultimately dispel doubts that have an intellectual basis.

11. Safeguard Against False Teachings

One of the risks of spiritual isolation is the vulnerability to false teachings. A grounded community serves as a protective measure against heresies that can instigate doubt. It upholds orthodoxy and ensures that teachings align with Scripture.

The battle against doubt is not one that needs to be, or should be, fought alone. The Christian community is a God-ordained resource for spiritual growth and fortification against the arrows of doubt. Whether it's through emotional support, collective worship, intellectual discussion, or service, the community offers multifaceted resources to maintain and strengthen our faith. Indeed, it is often through this web of relationships that God reminds us of His sovereignty, teaching us to depend on Him rather than attempting to walk on our own.

CHAPTER 6: Your Feelings Don't Have to Control You (Prayer as Rational Self-Talk)

Emotional Intelligence from a Christian Perspective

In an era where "feelings" often take center stage, it's important for Christians to grasp a Biblical understanding of emotions. Emotional intelligence, the ability to understand, manage, and effectively express one's emotions, is not contrary to Christian teachings; rather, it's an essential part of spiritual maturity. In this chapter, we'll explore how prayer serves as rational self-talk that aids emotional intelligence, enabling believers to live in freedom rather than being controlled by emotions.

1. The Nature of Emotions in the Bible

Scripture doesn't dismiss emotions. Jesus Himself experienced a range of emotions: compassion (Matthew 9:36), anger (John 2:15-17), and sorrow (Luke 22:44). Emotions are not inherently evil but can be misleading or manipulated (Jeremiah 17:9).

2. Emotions and The Fall

While emotions are part of God's design, they have been corrupted by the Fall. This corruption manifests as exaggerated feelings, impulsiveness, and the inability to properly regulate emotions. This is a manifestation of human independence from God's sovereignty and underlines the inherent flaw in human nature.

3. The Rationality of Prayer

Prayer can be viewed as rational self-talk—a dialogue with God that aligns our thoughts and feelings with His will. Philippians 4:6-7 tells us to present our requests to God through prayer, which leads to "the peace of God, which surpasses all understanding." When we pray, we are not just emotionally venting but inviting God's rationality into our emotional chaos.

4. Emotional Intelligence and Self-Control

Self-control, a fruit of the Spirit (Galatians 5:22-23), is closely related to emotional intelligence. Through prayer and engaging with the Scriptures, we can develop self-control that allows us to manage our emotions effectively.

5. Cognitive Behavioral Therapy (CBT) and Biblical Wisdom

While CBT, a form of psychotherapy, advocates for challenging one's distorted thoughts and beliefs, Scripture had long before advocated for the renewal of the mind (Romans 12:2). The practice of scrutinizing our thoughts through the lens of Scripture is a powerful way to develop emotional intelligence.

6. The Community Factor

The Christian community plays a crucial role in emotional intelligence. Accountability, mentorship, and discipleship within the Church can guide an individual in making emotionally intelligent decisions based on Biblical principles.

7. Emotional Regulation through Scriptural Meditation

The consistent meditation on Scripture can provide a stabilizing influence on our emotions. When David was deeply troubled, he meditated on the law of the Lord (Psalm 119:23). Through the Word, we can direct our emotions toward Godly action rather than being led astray by them.

8. Emotional Validation vs. Emotional Indulgence

It's important to make a distinction between validating one's emotions and indulging in them. Jesus validated His emotions through prayer in Gethsemane but did not let them divert Him from His mission. We can acknowledge our feelings without becoming enslaved to them.

9. Discerning the Spirit Behind Emotions

First Thessalonians 5:21-22 advises us to "test everything; hold fast what is good." Not all emotions come from the Holy Spirit. They can also arise from our sinful nature or external influences. Spiritual discernment is necessary to separate what is of God from what is not.

10. Accepting Human Limitations and Embracing God's Sovereignty

We must accept that we are not in ultimate control of our lives or our feelings. In the face of this limitation, prayer enables us to surrender our emotional burdens to God, acknowledging His sovereignty. This acceptance can bring emotional relief and spiritual growth, serving as an object lesson in recognizing our human inadequacy apart from God.

11. Role of Suffering in Emotional Intelligence

Suffering and emotional turmoil, while not designed by God for character development, serve as reminders of our limitations and inadequacies. Through these experiences, we learn the valuable lesson that emotional stability can only be achieved through reliance on God's sovereignty.

Being a Christian doesn't mean suppressing or ignoring emotions but managing them through the wisdom found in Scripture and prayer. By aligning our emotional life with Biblical principles and relying on the Christian community for support and guidance, we can cultivate emotional intelligence. This process helps us to better serve God and others, making us effective witnesses to the world that, in Christ, we can be free from the tyranny of unchecked emotions. Prayer serves as a powerful tool in this journey, aligning us with the rational mind of God and freeing us from the chaos of emotional bondage.

Identifying Destructive Emotional Patterns

Recognizing the role that emotions play in our lives is crucial for spiritual growth and healthy interactions with others. While emotions are God-given, they have been corrupted due to human sinfulness, making them unreliable guides for decision-making and behavior. This chapter focuses on identifying destructive emotional patterns and how a relationship with God through prayer and Scripture can help rectify them.

1. Understanding Destructive Emotional Patterns

Destructive emotional patterns often arise from negative thought cycles, bad habits, and recurring sins. They may manifest as constant worry, fear, jealousy, or uncontrollable anger. These patterns point to an underlying issue—human independence from God's sovereignty.

2. Scriptural Diagnosis of Destructive Emotions

Scripture provides ample guidance on identifying destructive emotions. Galatians 5:19-21 lists the "works of the flesh," which include "fits of anger, rivalries, dissensions, divisions, envy," and more. When these emotions dominate your life, they become destructive emotional patterns.

3. The Consequences of Destructive Emotional Patterns

Unchecked emotional patterns can lead to estranged relationships, poor decision-making, and spiritual stagnation. For instance, King Saul's jealousy led him down a path of ruin (1 Samuel 18:8-9). These emotions not only destroy us but also have ripple effects on those around us.

4. The Sin Factor

Destructive emotions are not just psychological issues but are rooted in sin. For example, uncontrolled anger can be traced back to pride or self-centeredness. James 4:1-2 tells us that quarrels and fights come from our desires that battle within us. We must address the sin to truly break free from the cycle.

5. The Role of Prayer in Identifying Emotional Patterns

Prayer serves as a mirror for our souls. In speaking honestly with God, we gain insights into our emotional state. David's Psalms often start with raw emotion but transition into reflections grounded in God's character. Prayer enables us to bring our emotional mess before God for His rational clarity.

6. Scriptural Meditation for Emotional Healing

Meditating on Scripture can help identify and rectify emotional flaws. For example, meditating on Philippians 4:8 directs us to focus on what is true, honorable, just, pure, lovely, and commendable, offering a way out of negative emotional loops.

7. Repentance and Realignment

Identifying the sin behind the emotion calls for repentance. This is not merely feeling sorry but involves a change of mind and behavior.

Repentance aligns our will with God's, as we make a conscious choice to avoid the emotional pitfalls that ensnare us.

8. The Role of Christian Community

Accountability within a Christian community can be instrumental in breaking free from destructive patterns. By sharing our struggles and seeking counsel, we place ourselves in a position to receive Godly wisdom and prayer support.

9. Suffering as a Signal

While suffering is not designed by God to build character, it often illuminates destructive emotional patterns. Suffering, in this context, becomes an object lesson revealing our need for dependence on God.

10. Long-term Strategies for Emotional Health

Breaking destructive emotional patterns is not a quick fix but a journey. Regular Bible study, continuous prayer, and community involvement are long-term strategies for achieving emotional health.

11. God's Sovereignty as the Ultimate Solution

At the heart of destructive emotional patterns is the denial of God's sovereignty. Accepting God's sovereignty means understanding that our feelings do not define reality—God does. When we accept this, we find that destructive emotional patterns lose their hold on us.

12. Real-world Examples and Testimonies

Consider the testimonies of those who have overcome destructive emotional patterns through faith. Such accounts serve as powerful reminders of how reliance on God can bring emotional freedom.

Identifying and rectifying destructive emotional patterns is an integral part of Christian maturity. Through prayer, repentance, and the engagement of Christian community, we can break the cycle of destructive emotions. This transformative process underlines the importance of acknowledging God's sovereignty over every aspect of our lives, including our emotional well-being. Thus, when we rely on God's sovereign guidance rather than our flawed emotional compass, we make meaningful strides towards emotional and spiritual health.

Scriptural Teachings on Emotional Management

The management of emotions is not a modern idea brought to us by self-help books or therapeutic methodologies; it is deeply rooted in biblical teaching. The Scripture provides wisdom for identifying, understanding, and managing our emotions in a way that honors God and benefits us and others around us. This chapter seeks to dive into the biblical worldview on emotional management.

1. The Emotional Landscape of the Bible

The Bible is not a stoic book; it is filled with real people experiencing a wide range of emotions. From David's lament to Paul's joy, the emotional range displayed illustrates the complexity of human experience.

2. God's Emotions

Understanding God's emotions helps us frame our own. Jehovah God is depicted as a Being with emotions, such as love, compassion, and even righteous anger. While God's emotions are perfect, ours are tainted by sin. The difference helps us to understand that emotions aren't inherently wrong, but they can be mismanaged.

3. The Wisdom of Proverbs

Proverbs contains practical wisdom on managing emotions. For example, "A soft answer turns away wrath, but a harsh word stirs up anger" (Proverbs 15:1 ESV). Emotional wisdom involves measured responses and thoughtful interaction with others.

4. Emotional Self-Control as a Fruit of the Spirit

Galatians 5:22-23 lists self-control as one of the fruits of the Spirit. Emotional management is a part of self-control. Fruits of the Spirit are not naturally occurring traits but are developed through living according to God's Word.

5. Jesus as Our Model

Jesus exhibited perfect emotional management. When tempted, slandered, and even crucified, He responded not out of raw emotion but in accordance with the Father's will. His example is our ideal model for emotional conduct.

6. Paul's Teachings on Emotional Management

Paul wrote extensively on this subject. In Philippians 4:6-7, he advises believers not to be anxious but to let their requests be known to God through prayer and supplication. Paul practiced what he preached, maintaining his joy and focus even in prison.

7. Prayer as Rational Self-Talk

Prayer is often a time where we can have "rational self-talk," bringing our emotions under the lens of Scriptural truth. In Psalm 42, the psalmist speaks to his soul, questioning why he is disquieted and encouraging hope in God.

8. The Psalms: A School for Emotional Management

The Psalms serve as a guide for how to bring our emotions before God. David and other psalmists do not shy away from expressing their feelings but always place them in the larger context of God's character and promises.

9. The Role of Suffering in Emotional Management

While suffering isn't designed by God to build our character, it often acts as an object lesson, making us realize our emotions are untrustworthy guides when compared to the unchanging character of God. Suffering unveils our need to depend on God's sovereignty.

10. Emotional Management in the Life of the Church

The body of Christ serves as a supportive community where emotional wisdom can be practiced and learned. "Bear one another's burdens, and so fulfill the law of Christ" (Galatians 6:2 ESV). It is within this framework that emotional management can truly thrive.

11. Dangers of Emotionalism

Scripture warns against making decisions based solely on feelings. Jeremiah 17:9 notes that the heart is deceitful above all things. An emotional faith is an unstable faith, and we are admonished to build our life upon the rock of Christ (Matthew 7:24-27).

12. Emotional Management and God's Sovereignty

Understanding the sovereignty of God forms the backbone of effective emotional management. When we understand that God is in control, even when our emotions are in turmoil, it brings a peace that surpasses all understanding (Philippians 4:7).

Scripture offers a well-rounded approach to emotional management. It acknowledges the reality and importance of emotions, while also setting boundaries to prevent emotions from leading us astray. By adopting the biblical model of emotional management—anchored in prayer and community, informed by Scriptural wisdom, and always conscious of God's sovereignty—we can experience emotional stability while giving glory to God.

The Role of Prayer in Emotional Wellness

In an age when emotional well-being is highly discussed and promoted, it's essential to look at this topic from a Scriptural perspective. A cornerstone of emotional wellness in a Christian context is prayer. Prayer is not merely a ritual; it is our direct line of communication with Jehovah, the Creator of our emotions. This chapter aims to dissect the role of prayer in achieving and maintaining emotional wellness.

1. Prayer as an Emotional Outlet

First, it's crucial to understand that prayer offers an emotional outlet. Rather than bottling up emotions, we can pour out our hearts to God. "Cast your burden on the Lord, and he will sustain you" (Psalm 55:22 ESV). In this way, prayer serves as a safety valve for emotional pressure.

2. Prayer for Discernment

As Christians, we need to differentiate between emotions that are legitimate and those that are not. Prayer helps us in discerning the feelings that align with God's Word from those that do not. "If any of you lacks wisdom, let him ask God, who gives generously to all without reproach, and it will be given him" (James 1:5 ESV).

3. Prayer as a Centering Mechanism

Prayer can act as an emotional "reset button," helping us refocus on God's will for our lives. Paul writes, "Do not be anxious about anything, but in everything by prayer and supplication with thanksgiving let your requests be made known to God" (Philippians 4:6 ESV).

4. Prayer as a Form of Rational Self-Talk

Prayer can serve as rational self-talk where we remind ourselves of the truths contained in Scripture. In doing so, we can counter the lies that our emotions sometimes tell us. We "take captive every thought to make it obedient to Christ" (2 Corinthians 10:5 ESV).

5. Prayer in Times of Suffering

While it is essential to note that God didn't design suffering to build character, suffering often exposes our emotional vulnerability. Prayer in times of suffering is a way to refocus on God's sovereignty, understanding that we are not in control but God is. Such realization can bring emotional relief.

6. Confession and Emotional Well-Being

The act of confession in prayer also contributes to emotional wellness. Holding onto sin leads to emotional and spiritual strain. David speaks of the joy of confession and forgiveness in Psalm 32, where he discusses the emotional turmoil of unconfessed sin and the relief that comes from reconciliation with God.

7. Thanksgiving in Prayer

A spirit of gratitude is known to improve emotional well-being. Paul encourages believers to "give thanks in all circumstances; for this is the will of God in Christ Jesus for you" (1 Thessalonians 5:18 ESV). Regularly thanking God in prayer reminds us of His goodness and can shift our emotional focus away from our issues and onto His providence.

8. Intercessory Prayer for Others

Praying for others shifts the focus away from our emotional state and toward the well-being of others. It allows us to participate in God's work and often provides a perspective that elevates our emotional well-being.

9. The Limitations of Prayer in Emotional Wellness

Prayer is a tool for emotional wellness, but it is not a magical solution to emotional or mental health issues. It is a part of a holistic approach that may also include counseling, community support, and sometimes medication. While prayer aligns us with God's will, it does not negate the necessity for other forms of treatment when required.

10. The Object Lesson of Human Suffering

Emotional wellness is not an end unto itself but can serve as an object lesson, making us realize our flawed human tendencies to be independent of God's sovereignty. By coming to Jehovah in prayer, we acknowledge our limitations and His ultimate control over all things, which can bring emotional peace.

11. Prayer in Community

The church should be a place where emotional wellness is fostered through communal prayer. James 5:16 tells us to "confess your sins to one another and pray for one another, that you may be healed" (ESV). This mutual intercession and accountability can be emotionally therapeutic.

12. The Final Word on Prayer and Emotional Wellness

While the modern world offers various strategies for emotional well-being, none are as holistic and eternally meaningful as a life of prayer. It brings our emotions under the Lordship of Christ, enabling us to live emotionally balanced lives for God's glory.

Prayer plays a pivotal role in emotional wellness, serving as an emotional outlet, a discernment tool, and a means of focusing on God's sovereignty. Through prayer, we can manage our emotions in a way that aligns with Scriptural principles and brings glory to God. We learn that emotional wellness is not merely about feeling good but about aligning our feelings with God's eternal truths.

CHAPTER 7: The Power of Forgiveness in Overcoming Pain

Biblical Principles of Forgiveness

The topic of forgiveness is a cornerstone in Christian ethics and emotional well-being. Holding onto grudges, anger, or resentment often yields a type of emotional suffering that can become a lifelong burden. This chapter aims to unpack the Scriptural teachings on forgiveness as a powerful tool in overcoming emotional and relational pain.

1. The Command to Forgive

Jesus Christ makes it abundantly clear that forgiveness is not optional for those who follow Him. He instructs us to forgive "seventy-seven times," illustrating that there should be no limit to our forgiveness (Matthew 18:22 ESV). Failure to forgive others results in hindrances to our relationship with God (Matthew 6:14-15).

2. The Model of God's Forgiveness

God forgave humanity's sin through the sacrificial death and resurrection of Jesus Christ. Ephesians 4:32 says, "Be kind to one another, tenderhearted, forgiving one another, as God in Christ forgave you" (ESV). This is the ultimate model of forgiveness we are to emulate.

3. Forgiveness as Emotional Freedom

Harboring resentment and unforgiveness often ties us to the very pain we wish to overcome. Forgiveness liberates us emotionally, enabling us to move forward in life without being shackled by past hurts.

4. The Complexity of Forgiveness

While Scripture encourages forgiveness, it doesn't deny the complexity and difficulty of the process. It can be a long, emotionally draining endeavor, especially when dealing with deep-seated hurts or betrayal.

5. Forgiveness and Justice

Forgiveness does not mean overlooking justice. It is possible to forgive while still pursuing justice, especially in cases that involve abuse, criminal activity, or any form of exploitation. The Apostle Paul makes it clear that civil authorities are "God's servant for your good" (Romans 13:4 ESV).

6. Forgiveness in Times of Suffering

While God didn't design suffering for personal growth, experiencing pain often becomes a crucible where our ability to forgive is tested. Understanding the object lesson of human suffering and God's sovereignty helps us recognize our limited perspective and the importance of aligning our will with His.

7. Forgiveness and Reconciliation

Forgiveness may pave the way for reconciliation, but they are not the same. Reconciliation requires the willing participation of both parties and may not always be possible or advisable, especially in cases of ongoing harm or abuse.

8. Self-Forgiveness

One of the most challenging persons to forgive can be oneself. The principles of forgiveness apply not just to forgiving others but also to forgiving ourselves. This can be particularly difficult when we fail to live up to our own moral or spiritual expectations.

9. Setting Boundaries

Forgiveness doesn't equate to a lack of boundaries. It is possible to forgive someone and still maintain distance if they continue in a pattern of harmful behavior. "Above all else, guard your heart, for everything you do flows from it" (Proverbs 4:23 ESV).

10. The Role of Community in Forgiveness

Forgiving can be an extremely challenging task, often requiring the support and wisdom of other believers. The Christian community can provide accountability, wisdom, and encouragement in the journey towards forgiveness.

11. The Link Between Forgiveness and Peace

The act of forgiveness is intrinsically linked to experiencing peace. When Paul says, "Let the peace of Christ rule in your hearts," he links this to being thankful and letting the "word of Christ dwell in you richly" (Colossians 3:15-16 ESV).

12. The Paradox of Forgiveness

The power of forgiveness lies in its paradox: by giving up our right to retaliation or holding a grudge, we gain emotional and spiritual freedom. When we let go, we actually gain more than we could ever imagine.

Forgiveness is not merely a religious principle but a lifestyle choice that has profound implications for emotional well-being and spiritual maturity. While forgiving others can be an arduous process, the teachings of Scripture provide us with the framework and motivation to do so. Forgiveness should be viewed not merely as an act but as a transformative process, one that draws us closer to the very heart of God and helps us navigate the intricate emotional landscape of human relationships. It can also serve as an object lesson, illustrating our dependence on God's sovereignty and wisdom in dealing with the complexities of human interaction and emotional well-being.

The Psychological and Spiritual Benefits of Forgiving

Forgiveness is often considered a theological concept, exclusively within the domain of spiritual teaching. However, forgiveness intersects deeply with our psychological well-being. This chapter aims to elucidate the psychological and spiritual benefits of forgiveness, emphasizing how these two aspects often intertwine in a symbiotic relationship.

1. Psychological Liberation

One of the most immediate psychological benefits of forgiveness is a sense of liberation. Holding onto anger, bitterness, or resentment has been linked to stress, insomnia, and even physical ailments. When we forgive, we shed these toxic emotions and give room for peace and joy to thrive.

2. Reduced Anxiety and Depression

The act of forgiveness has been shown to alleviate symptoms of anxiety and depression. Harboring negative emotions towards others or oneself can act as a significant emotional drain. When you forgive, you free up emotional energy that can be better invested in constructive activities and relationships.

3. Enhanced Self-Esteem

When we find it within ourselves to forgive, it also impacts our self-esteem. Understanding that we have the power to break free from the chains of the past fosters a sense of self-empowerment.

4. Spiritual Elevation

From a spiritual standpoint, forgiveness elevates our relationship with God. When we forgive others, we align ourselves with God's nature of unconditional love and mercy. The Apostle Paul wrote, "Be kind to one another, tenderhearted, forgiving one another, as God in Christ forgave you" (Ephesians 4:32, ESV).

5. Openness to Divine Guidance

Unforgiveness can act as a barrier to our openness to divine guidance through the inspired Word of God. Forgiving allows us to clear the emotional clutter, making us more receptive to the teachings and guidance of Scripture.

6. Cultivation of the Fruits of the Spirit

Forgiveness is consistent with the cultivation of the Fruits of the Spirit described in Galatians 5:22-23. It aligns with love, joy, peace, patience, kindness, goodness, faithfulness, gentleness, and self-control.

7. Suffering as an Object Lesson

While God didn't create suffering for personal development, the experience of being wronged and the subsequent need for forgiveness often serves as an object lesson. It illuminates the flaws of human independence from God's sovereignty and reveals our limitations in managing our own emotional well-being.

8. Disconnection from Cycles of Retribution

One of the overlooked benefits of forgiveness is the discontinuation of cycles of retribution and violence. The Old Testament often speaks about the cycle of sin and its consequences. Forgiveness allows for a new beginning, a break in the cycle that could otherwise perpetuate indefinitely.

9. Improved Interpersonal Relationships

Forgiveness often improves the quality of our interpersonal relationships. Whether within families, among friends, or in marriage, the act of forgiving paves the way for more authentic and loving interactions.

10. Longevity and Physical Health

While it may seem surprising, there is research to suggest that forgiveness can contribute to physical health. Emotional stress, often a by-product of unforgiveness, has been linked to various health problems, from heart disease to a weakened immune system.

11. Increased Resilience

Another psychological benefit is increased resilience. Life will inevitably present us with more situations where forgiveness is needed. The act of forgiving can be seen as emotional training, increasing our resilience against future emotional upheavals.

12. Alignment with Christ's Teaching and Example

Ultimately, forgiving aligns us with the teachings and example of Jesus Christ, who forgave even those who crucified Him. "Father, forgive them, for they know not what they do," He said (Luke 23:34, ESV). This is the ultimate example of forgiveness and a stark illustration of the kind of love God wishes to cultivate in our hearts.

Forgiveness is not a mere moral obligation but a life-affirming choice with tangible psychological and spiritual benefits. Embracing forgiveness can lead to emotional freedom, greater mental well-being, and a deeper, more intimate relationship with God. While it does not negate the justice system or the consequences of actions, it allows us to navigate the complex landscape of human interactions with greater wisdom and serenity. When we forgive, we echo God's grace, and in doing so, we draw closer to Him and further away from the pitfalls of a life marked by resentment and unforgiveness.

Overcoming the Barriers to Forgiveness

The journey towards forgiveness can be tumultuous, riddled with emotional and psychological roadblocks. As much as we know the benefits of forgiving, the act often seems Herculean. This chapter aims to dissect these barriers and provide strategies for overcoming them within a framework of conservative Christian counseling.

1. The Desire for Justice

A significant roadblock to forgiveness is the inherent desire for justice. When someone has wronged us, our initial reaction is often to seek retribution. However, it's crucial to distinguish between justice and vengeance. While God is a God of justice, He also teaches forgiveness. Romans 12:19 says, "Beloved, never avenge yourselves, but leave it to the wrath of God, for it is written, 'Vengeance is mine, I will repay, says the Lord'" (ESV).

2. Emotional Scars

Long-standing emotional wounds can harden into scars that act as barriers to forgiveness. Emotional healing may require time, prayer, and even professional counseling. However, one can take solace in the redemptive power of Christ, who came to "bind up the brokenhearted" (Isaiah 61:1, ESV).

3. Pride and Ego

Our pride can be a significant stumbling block in the journey toward forgiveness. The need to maintain a self-image of being wronged can be more satisfying to the ego than the freedom that comes with forgiveness. However, Scripture teaches us that pride comes before a fall (Proverbs 16:18, ESV), and thus it's essential to confront and humble our ego for the sake of our spiritual health.

4. Lack of Scriptural Understanding

The absence of a Scriptural framework for understanding forgiveness can also be a barrier. It is crucial to immerse ourselves in the teachings of the Bible to understand God's perspective on forgiveness, modeled perfectly through the life and sacrifice of Jesus Christ.

5. The Illusion of Control

Sometimes, holding onto a grudge gives us the illusion of control over a situation or individual. This is a fallacy. In fact, unforgiveness chains us to the past and to the individual who has wronged us. We gain true control and freedom only when we forgive.

6. Suffering as an Object Lesson

The pain we experience, while not orchestrated by God, serves as a life lesson about the limitations of human capabilities apart from the divine will. God allows this suffering to reveal our insufficiency in managing life's challenges independently of Him. It serves as an object lesson teaching us about God's sovereignty and our need for His guidance in overcoming emotional challenges like unforgiveness.

7. Fears and Insecurities

The fear of being hurt again often acts as a significant deterrent to forgiveness. While these fears are entirely human, they can be managed through prayer and Scripture. 2 Timothy 1:7 reminds us, "for God gave us a spirit not of fear but of power and love and self-control" (ESV).

8. External Influences

Sometimes, society, culture, or even well-meaning friends can discourage us from forgiving, equating it with weakness. Such external influences can be significant barriers to forgiveness but should be evaluated critically against the truth of Scripture.

9. Complexity of Human Emotion

Human emotions are complex and layered. Anger, resentment, and bitterness often coexist with love, empathy, and a desire for reconciliation. Navigating this emotional labyrinth requires spiritual wisdom and possibly counsel from trusted Christians who stand firm on biblical truth.

10. Theological Misunderstandings

Misinterpretations or lack of understanding of theological concepts can impede the act of forgiveness. It's crucial to grasp that while God is a God of justice, He is also a God of immense mercy and grace.

11. Impatience for Emotional Resolution

Many people expect emotional resolution to come immediately after they decide to forgive. However, forgiveness is often a process. It's essential to extend grace to ourselves during this journey, just as God extends His grace to us.

12. Misperceptions of Forgiveness

Many assume that to forgive is to forget or to condone the action. This is a misperception. Forgiveness is not about forgetting or condoning but freeing oneself from the bondage of bitterness and opening oneself up to God's healing power.

Overcoming the barriers to forgiveness is an intricate journey that requires spiritual fortitude, Scriptural wisdom, and a heart willing to align with God's will. Yet, the spiritual and psychological freedom that comes from forgiveness is invaluable. As we navigate these roadblocks, let us remember that God's grace is sufficient for us, and His power is made perfect in our weaknesses (2 Corinthians 12:9, ESV). Thus, leaning into God's strength can help us overcome these barriers and walk in the liberating path of forgiveness.

The Role of Repentance and Restitution

Forgiveness is a complex theological and psychological topic, and within its broad landscape exists the role of repentance and restitution. These elements often serve as crucial steps in the process of achieving meaningful forgiveness, both in our relationship with God and in our interpersonal relationships. This chapter aims to unpack the biblical principles that underline the importance of repentance and restitution in the context of forgiveness.

Repentance: The First Step

In Scripture, repentance is portrayed as a prerequisite to divine forgiveness. The process starts with recognizing our sinfulness, feeling remorse, and then turning away from sin toward God. Repentance is an essential part of genuine forgiveness and spiritual growth. Acts 3:19 (ESV) says, "Repent therefore, and turn back, that your sins may be blotted out."

Restitution: Making Amends

While repentance deals with the spiritual and psychological state of a person, restitution focuses on the external actions that aim to "right the wrong" whenever possible. It is about making amends, compensating for the loss, or restoring what was broken. Numbers 5:7 (ESV) states, "He shall confess his sin that he has committed. And he shall make full restitution for his wrong, adding a fifth to it and giving it to him to whom he did the wrong."

Repentance in Interpersonal Relationships

When dealing with offenses in interpersonal relationships, true repentance will manifest in sincere apologies and a commitment to refrain from future transgressions. Merely saying "I'm sorry" is insufficient if not accompanied by a change in behavior. Repentance fosters trust, an essential ingredient in any healthy relationship.

The Role of Restitution in Interpersonal Forgiveness

Restitution in human relationships, much like its biblical counterpart, involves taking steps to redress the wrongs done. Depending on the nature of the offense, this could mean returning stolen property, publicly apologizing for a public offense, or engaging in acts of service to make amends.

Caveats in Restitution

While restitution is a noble aim, it is not always possible or even advisable to make amends for every offense. Some wounds cannot be easily mended, and attempts to do so may even exacerbate the situation. Wisdom and discernment, often gained through prayer and counsel from trusted believers, are crucial in these instances.

Repentance, Restitution, and God's Sovereignty

Even though suffering was not designed by God, it is crucial to understand that mankind's failings and hardships often stem from a deviation from God's will. This is the very essence of sin from which we repent. Our suffering serves as an object lesson allowed by God to teach humanity about the dire consequences of acting independently of His divine sovereignty.

Emotional Barriers to Repentance and Restitution

Fear, pride, and denial are often the emotional barriers that hinder us from taking the steps of repentance and restitution. While it's difficult to confront our failings, it is only through this discomfort that true spiritual growth can occur.

Unrepentance and Unforgiveness

Failure to repent not only affects our relationship with God but also places a burden on our interpersonal relationships. It hinders the process of forgiveness and may cause lasting emotional and spiritual damage.

The Liberation of Repentance and Restitution

Both repentance and restitution free us from the chains of guilt and shame. In fact, these steps offer both the offender and the offended a pathway toward emotional and spiritual liberation, aligning their wills more closely with God's.

The Church's Role

The church should be a community that encourages both repentance and restitution. The church's role is to guide, counsel, and provide a framework within which these biblical principles can be exercised fruitfully.

Practical Steps

1. **Self-examination:** Constant self-examination is necessary for recognizing the need for repentance and restitution.
2. **Seeking Counsel:** Wisdom from mature Christians can provide valuable insights into whether and how to make restitution.

3. **Prayer:** Prayer is indispensable for asking for God's guidance in the complex journey of repentance and restitution.

The journey of forgiveness is both intricate and beautiful. It is a journey that requires the courage to repent and make restitution. These are not merely acts that relieve guilt, but transformative practices that align us more closely with God's character and His will for our lives. These principles serve as conduits for healing, channels of grace, and pathways to a deeper relationship with God and our fellow man. They are integral to the fabric of Christian ethics, painting a vivid picture of the gospel's transformative power. Through repentance and restitution, we witness the beauty of grace, the relief of liberation, and the warmth of restored relationships.

CHAPTER 8: The Problem of Suffering in the Old Testament

The Story of Job: An Examination

The story of Job is perhaps the most profound biblical narrative dealing with the problem of human suffering. Though many people turn to the Book of Job seeking answers, they often walk away with even more questions. But could it be that the story is meant to foster a different type of understanding, one that underscores the mystery and majesty of God's sovereignty rather than providing direct answers to why we suffer?

Job: A Righteous Man

The account begins by establishing Job as a man of integrity and righteousness. Job 1:1 (ESV) states, "There was a man in the land of Uz whose name was Job, and that man was blameless and upright, one who feared God and turned away from evil." This is significant because it negates the argument that suffering is always a result of personal sin.

The Heavenly Debate

Job's suffering begins when Satan challenges his righteousness in the heavenly courts. Satan suggests that Job's piety is merely a result of his prosperity and that if his blessings were taken away, he would curse God. Jehovah allows this affliction to befall Job but sets limitations, demonstrating His ultimate sovereignty over the entire situation. This reflects how God allows suffering as a larger object lesson about His sovereignty and the human inability to walk independently of it.

Job's Afflictions

Job loses his wealth, his children, and is stricken with painful sores. Through all these calamities, Job does not sin by charging God with wrongdoing (Job 1:22). However, as his suffering deepens, he wrestles with despair and questions God's justice.

The Counsel of Friends

Job's friends insist that he must have committed a grievous sin to warrant such suffering. Their flawed theology assumes a straightforward relationship between sin and suffering, failing to consider the complex dynamics involving God's sovereignty.

Jehovah Speaks

The climax of the book comes when God Himself speaks out of the whirlwind. Instead of providing direct answers, He overwhelms Job with a series of questions that showcase His omnipotence and wisdom. Jehovah doesn't explain the "why" behind Job's suffering but redirects the focus to Who is in control.

Job's Restoration

In the end, Job repents for questioning God's justice. He is subsequently restored and blessed even more abundantly than before. This, however, should not be seen as a formula for how God deals with human suffering; it is merely the conclusion of this specific narrative.

The Sovereignty of God and Human Suffering

The Book of Job does not explain why good people suffer but rather points us toward the One who governs the universe in wisdom and righteousness. God doesn't design suffering but allows it to demonstrate the inherent flaw in human independence from His sovereignty. The story teaches us that even when we don't have all the answers, we can still trust in God's character.

Theological Implications

1. **Suffering Is Complex:** Job's story teaches us that the dynamics of suffering are complex and not always directly linked to individual sin.

2. **God's Sovereignty:** Jehovah's dialogue with Satan and His limitations on Job's suffering assert His ultimate control over all circumstances.

3. **Human Limitations:** The narrative makes it clear that humanity does not possess the capacity to fully understand God's reasons for allowing suffering.

Emotional Responses and Coping

While Job questioned and lamented, he never lost his faith. His emotional turmoil was not a lack of faith but an authentic wrestling with realities that seemed contradictory. This resonates with many who suffer, providing a scriptural model for how to maintain faith in times of inexplicable suffering.

The story of Job serves as a profound, if perplexing, text regarding the problem of suffering. It calls us to trust in God's sovereignty, even when we don't understand our circumstances. It challenges simplistic theological equations that equate suffering with sin and prosperity with righteousness. Instead, it forces us to grapple with the inherent complexity and mystery of a world governed by an infinitely wise and sovereign God. Job's story concludes on a hopeful note, not by answering all questions, but by restoring the focus on Jehovah, who is greater than any dilemma we may encounter, including suffering.

Israel's Suffering and Jehovah's Plan

The narrative of Israel as portrayed in the Old Testament provides a rich tapestry for examining the complex issue of suffering. It is not just the story of one man or a family, but an entire nation that faces trials, oppression, and divine discipline. Like the story of Job, the experience of Israel serves to teach us much about God's sovereignty and how human suffering fits within that overarching narrative.

A Nation Chosen but Tested

Israel was chosen by Jehovah to be a "kingdom of priests and a holy nation" (Exodus 19:6, ESV). This divine selection, however, was not a guarantee against hardship. Right from the time of their enslavement in Egypt to their exile in Babylon, the Israelites faced numerous instances of suffering.

The Object Lesson: Egypt

The suffering of the Israelites in Egypt was not designed by God but allowed to occur under His sovereignty. Jehovah allowed Israel's enslavement and eventual liberation as an object lesson for humanity. It displayed His power, His justice, and His faithfulness. However, the suffering itself was not engineered by God; rather, it unfolded in a world where human choices have real consequences.

Wilderness Wanderings: Discipline and Dependency

After their liberation, the Israelites wandered in the wilderness for 40 years. While the journey was replete with trials, it was also an education in dependency on Jehovah. The wilderness period was a learning curve for a nation that needed to trust Jehovah wholeheartedly.

Divine Discipline: The Exile

The Babylonian Exile represents perhaps the most profound collective suffering experienced by Israel. Yet even here, Jehovah's sovereignty is evident. God had warned Israel through the prophets, like Isaiah and Jeremiah, about the dire consequences of their disobedience. When the suffering came, it was not arbitrary but a part of divine discipline.

Israel's Misunderstandings

One common misunderstanding the Israelites had was thinking their chosen status immunized them against hardship. They often questioned God's goodness and justice during their suffering, similar to Job's friends who assumed a direct correlation between suffering and personal sin. Yet, Jehovah consistently upended this paradigm by displaying that the issue was far more complex.

A Broader Theological Framework

1. **Divine Sovereignty:** Israel's history makes it clear that Jehovah is in ultimate control, even when His people go through unimaginable suffering. His promises never fail, even though the road to their fulfillment is often fraught with hardship.
2. **Human Agency:** Just as Israel had a role to play in their own destiny, individuals have the capacity for free will. This will can either align with God's or deviate from it, leading to suffering.
3. **Restorative Justice:** God's justice is not solely punitive but aims for restoration and redemption, as seen in the return from the Exile.

Emotional and Spiritual Responses

Israel's history contains a mix of faithful and faithless responses to suffering. Whether it was the rebellions recorded in Numbers or the heartfelt laments in the Psalms, Israel's experience tells us that suffering can be faced with either trust in Jehovah or misplaced self-reliance.

The experience of Israel in the Old Testament adds another layer of complexity to the biblical understanding of suffering. It highlights that suffering can arise from various factors such as discipline, the consequences of collective sin, or from living in a fallen world. However, the overarching lesson is that God's sovereignty is constant throughout. Jehovah's dealings with Israel are part of a grand object lesson in understanding that human suffering can neither be fully understood nor should it be trivialized. Rather, it serves as a poignant reminder of the urgency to align oneself with God's ultimate plans and purposes, learning to fully rely on His sovereignty.

Lessons from the Psalms: The Language of Lament

The Psalms are often considered the emotional heartbeat of the Scriptures, encapsulating the full range of human experiences, emotions, and states of the soul. Among these, the language of lament is particularly instructive for anyone grappling with the problem of suffering. Understanding the role of lament in the Psalms offers valuable insights into the relationship between human suffering and divine sovereignty.

The Nature of Lament

Lament in the Psalms is a form of prayerful petition that arises from conditions of distress, grief, or sorrow. Contrary to some popular opinions that lament may signify a lack of faith, the Psalms reveal that lament is a genuine, permitted form of conversing with Jehovah. It is not a sign of weakness but a candid recognition of our frailty and dependence on God.

Elements of Lament in Psalms

1. **Address to Jehovah**: A lament usually begins by invoking God's name or attributes. Even in sorrow, the psalmists begin with the acknowledgment of God's sovereignty.
2. **Complaint**: The psalmists lay bare their predicaments, often with graphic descriptions of their suffering. This demonstrates that God invites us to be honest with Him.
3. **Petition**: The psalmists ask Jehovah for specific forms of intervention or relief.
4. **Expression of Trust**: Even in the depth of suffering, the psalmists usually express trust in Jehovah's goodness and sovereignty.
5. **Vow of Praise**: The lament often closes with a vow to praise Jehovah once the trial has ended, indicating a hope for the future based on God's character.

Lament as an Object Lesson

While God didn't design suffering for its own sake, He allows it as part of the larger object lesson teaching humanity about the limitations of human independence and the necessity of divine sovereignty. Lament, as encapsulated in the Psalms, exemplifies this. Through it, we learn the futility of self-reliance and the importance of turning to Jehovah.

Case Studies from the Psalms

1. **Psalm 13**: Here, the psalmist feels forgotten by God and beseeches Him for answers. Despite this, the psalm concludes with an affirmation of trust in Jehovah's steadfast love.
2. **Psalm 22**: This is a Messianic psalm where the language of intense suffering is evident. It exemplifies how even the most extreme suffering can be part of Jehovah's sovereign plan.

3. **Psalm 88**: One of the darkest psalms, it is almost entirely composed of lament. Remarkably, it doesn't conclude with an expression of hope or trust, suggesting that sometimes the experience of suffering is open-ended, yet this too is accommodated within the biblical tradition.

Emotional Responses and Lament

Lament allows for emotional honesty before God. Instead of suppressing their emotions, the psalmists pour out their hearts. Lament provides a structured way of dealing with emotional turmoil, placing it in the context of a relationship with Jehovah, who is sovereign even when we do not understand the specifics of His plan.

Practical Applications

1. **Freedom to Grieve**: Lament teaches us that it's acceptable to grieve and present our requests to Jehovah without restraint.

2. **Theological Resonance**: Even in suffering, understanding Jehovah's sovereignty gives depth to our lament. It allows us to vent while retaining our foundational beliefs.

3. **Emotional Balance**: Lament has a cathartic role, enabling us to bring our sorrows before Jehovah and then realigning our emotional state through expressions of trust and hope.

The Psalms give us a rich theology of lament, revealing that suffering, while not designed by Jehovah, is a circumstance He allows as part of an object lesson teaching humanity about the importance of His sovereignty. Lament is a constructive form of dealing with emotional turmoil, serving as a poignant reminder that we cannot walk on our own but need to consistently rely on Jehovah's guidance. Thus, the language of lament in the Psalms serves as a theological and emotional compass, helping us navigate the intricate pathways of human suffering while holding fast to the unchanging nature of divine sovereignty.

CHAPTER 9: What the New Testament Teaches About Suffering

Suffering as a Christian Virtue

The New Testament presents a nuanced perspective on the issue of suffering, often portraying it as a component of Christian living. However, we must clarify that while suffering is described in a way that may seem like a virtue, this does not mean Jehovah designed suffering for its own sake. Rather, He allows it as an object lesson to underline human limitations and the need for divine guidance and sovereignty.

Suffering in the Context of Christ

The most pivotal teaching on suffering comes from the life, death, and resurrection of Jesus Christ. His suffering was not a consequence of His actions but was allowed by Jehovah as a means to fulfill divine justice and bring about redemption (Isaiah 53:5; 1 Peter 2:24). Christ's suffering sets the paradigm for understanding suffering as a Christian virtue.

Apostolic Teachings on Suffering

1. **Pauline Epistles:** Paul often spoke of suffering as a reality for Christians (2 Timothy 3:12). He considered it a means by which believers share in the sufferings of Christ (Philippians 3:10).
2. **Peter's Perspective:** Peter views suffering as a part of the Christian life and a way to share in Christ's sufferings (1 Peter 4:13). He also indicates that suffering may occur for doing

good, thereby highlighting its potential virtuous nature (1 Peter 3:17).

3. **James's View:** James encourages believers to consider it "pure joy" when facing trials because the testing of faith produces perseverance (James 1:2-3).

Suffering and the Christian Virtues

1. **Endurance:** Trials and sufferings are meant to develop perseverance, enabling Christians to remain steadfast in their faith (Romans 5:3-4).

2. **Humility:** Suffering serves as a constant reminder of our need for Jehovah, as it was through Christ's humility that we have hope (Philippians 2:5-11).

3. **Compassion:** Having experienced suffering, Christians are better equipped to empathize with others who are going through similar struggles (2 Corinthians 1:3-4).

The Problem of Suffering Revisited

Suffering is not an objective good; it's a state allowed by Jehovah to teach humanity a lesson about the flaw inherent in our independence from Him. The New Testament, while recognizing the virtuous capabilities developed through suffering, doesn't negate its problematic nature but places it within the overarching framework of divine sovereignty and the narrative of redemption.

Christian Suffering and the Object Lesson

Since God allows suffering to demonstrate the limits of human independence, when Christians experience suffering and respond virtuously, they are participating in the broader object lesson meant for all of humanity. They showcase the necessity of relying on Jehovah for guidance, strength, and ultimate deliverance.

Suffering and the Kingdom of God

In the New Testament, suffering is also tied to the hope of the Kingdom of God. The "momentary troubles" are considered light compared to the eternal glory that awaits believers (2 Corinthians 4:17).

Case Studies in Suffering

1. **Stephen**: His martyrdom is an example of virtuous suffering, responding with forgiveness toward his persecutors (Acts 7:60).
2. **Apostle Paul**: Despite immense suffering, he found contentment in whatever circumstance, relying solely on Christ's strength (Philippians 4:11-13).

Practical Implications

1. **Comfort Through Scripture**: Meditating on God's promises can offer solace during challenging times (Romans 15:4).
2. **Prayer**: Prayer is an essential tool for emotional and spiritual stability in times of suffering (Philippians 4:6-7).
3. **Community Support**: A supportive Christian community can provide practical and emotional support (Galatians 6:2).

While the New Testament seems to elevate suffering to a virtue for Christians, it is essential to remember that Jehovah allows it as an object lesson to humanity. This suffering is not meaningless but serves as a poignant demonstration of the need for divine guidance and sovereignty in our lives. The manner in which Christians deal with suffering—by developing virtues such as endurance, humility, and compassion—serves to emphasize the need for reliance on Jehovah, whose ultimate plan involves the eradication of suffering and the establishment of His Kingdom.

Pauline Perspectives on Suffering

In the Pauline corpus, suffering emerges as a recurrent theme, offering profound insights into the nature, purpose, and response to affliction. This chapter focuses on Apostle Paul's teachings on suffering and situates it within the framework that God does not will suffering, but rather allows it to expose the inherent flaws in human independence from His sovereignty. Paul's perspectives serve as essential theological and practical guidance for Christians navigating trials.

Suffering and Paul's Own Life

Apostle Paul himself underwent extensive suffering for the cause of Christ—from beatings and imprisonment to shipwrecks and hunger (2 Corinthians 11:23-28). His experiences offer a lens through which we can understand suffering in the life of a believer.

Suffering as Participation in Christ's Afflictions

Paul speaks of suffering as sharing in the afflictions of Christ. "That I may know him and the power of his resurrection, and may share his sufferings, becoming like him in his death" (Philippians 3:10, ESV). This statement suggests that suffering serves to deepen our relationship with Christ. It's not that God orchestrates suffering for this purpose; rather, He allows it, and within that framework, suffering can serve as an opportunity to identify more closely with Christ.

Suffering and the Body of Christ

For Paul, individual suffering is not isolated but impacts the entire body of Christ (1 Corinthians 12:26). Our experiences of suffering, therefore, are not solely about us but also about our role and relationships within the body of Christ.

Suffering and Endurance

Paul links suffering with endurance and character, as seen in Romans 5:3-5. While God does not design suffering to build character or endurance, He allows it, and endurance can be a byproduct. In other words, the development of virtues like endurance is not the primary objective but can be a secondary outcome.

Suffering and Comfort

In 2 Corinthians 1:3-7, Paul introduces the idea that God comforts us in our afflictions so that we may comfort others. This comfort isn't a solution to suffering but a means to endure it. It's also a way to prepare us to be agents of comfort to others, thereby creating a community that reflects the compassion and care of Jehovah.

Suffering and Glory

Paul often contrasts present suffering with future glory. In Romans 8:18, he says, "For I consider that the sufferings of this present time are not worth comparing with the glory that is to be revealed to us" (ESV). While suffering is allowed by God to demonstrate human limitations and the need for His sovereignty, it also serves to heighten the Christian's longing for the eternal state where suffering will be no more.

Suffering and the Power of Christ

Paul's "thorn in the flesh" serves as a vivid example (2 Corinthians 12:7-10). Jehovah allows the suffering to continue, not to improve Paul's character, but to demonstrate that His grace is sufficient. The moment becomes an object lesson for Paul and others about human limitations and divine sufficiency.

Practical Responses to Suffering According to Paul

1. **Prayer and Supplication**: Philippians 4:6-7 recommends prayer as a means of acquiring peace during challenging times.
2. **Rely on Scripture**: Paul advises Timothy to rely on the sacred writings for teaching, reproof, correction, and training in righteousness (2 Timothy 3:16).
3. **Community**: Galatians 6:2 mentions carrying each other's burdens as a way to fulfill the law of Christ.

Paul's epistles offer a multifaceted perspective on suffering, accentuated by his own life experiences. Though Jehovah allows suffering, it can serve various secondary roles in the believer's life—from fostering a deeper communion with Christ to equipping us with endurance and comfort for ourselves and others. The core lesson, however, remains constant: suffering exposes the fundamental flaw in human autonomy and highlights the necessity for submission to divine sovereignty. We must remember that the virtues developed are not the end but rather the means to affirm our constant need for God.

The Ultimate Suffering: The Crucifixion of Christ

When discussing suffering within the New Testament framework, one cannot sidestep the crucifixion of Jesus Christ. The crucifixion is not merely an event of extreme physical suffering but represents a theological climax that unveils profound truths about sin, justice, redemption, and reconciliation. It is the fulcrum on which the salvation history pivots and a vivid example of how God allows suffering to serve His greater purposes.

The Nature of Christ's Suffering

The crucifixion is a horrific form of execution, involving indescribable pain and humiliation. Jesus endured not only physical torment but also the spiritual weight of human sin and divine wrath.

However, it is essential to understand that God didn't design this suffering but allowed it to unfold in the redemptive plan.

The Substitutionary Atonement

Christ's suffering on the cross serves as a substitute for the eternal suffering humanity deserves due to sin. "For Christ also suffered once for sins, the righteous for the unrighteous, that he might bring us to God" (1 Peter 3:18, ESV). His sacrifice satisfies divine justice, allowing God's mercy to extend toward repentant sinners.

The Exposition of Human Independence

The crucifixion exposes the consequence of human independence from God's sovereignty. The rulers, religious leaders, and crowds who called for Christ's crucifixion epitomize the inherent flaws in human judgment and autonomy. It becomes an object lesson for humanity about the dire implications of rejecting God's sovereignty.

The Vindication of Divine Justice

While God did not desire the suffering inherent in the crucifixion, He permitted it to demonstrate His justice. The death of Christ fulfills the requirement of the law that "the wages of sin is death" (Romans 6:23, ESV). God's justice and mercy intersect at the cross, making reconciliation possible for humanity.

Suffering and Love

God's allowing of this extreme form of suffering was not arbitrary but aimed at revealing His love for humanity. "For God so loved the world, that he gave his only Son, that whoever believes in him should not perish but have eternal life" (John 3:16, ESV). The crucifixion becomes a manifestation of divine love, even if it involves suffering that God merely permits rather than orchestrates.

The Model for Christian Suffering

The crucifixion offers an unparalleled model for Christian suffering. While God does not design suffering for Christian growth or endurance, Christ's example shows how to endure suffering while maintaining faith and integrity. "For to this you have been called, because Christ also suffered for you, leaving you an example, so that you might follow in his steps" (1 Peter 2:21, ESV).

Beyond Suffering: The Resurrection

The crucifixion story does not end in suffering but culminates in the resurrection. The resurrection confirms the efficacy of Christ's suffering and offers hope to believers that their own suffering is temporary and will be overcome in eternal life.

Practical Implications

1. **Reflection**: Christians can use Christ's crucifixion as a mirror to reflect on the severity of sin and the depth of God's love.

2. **Prayer**: The event should compel believers to pray for strength and wisdom to endure their own trials while holding fast to the hope of resurrection.

3. **Evangelism**: Understanding the enormity of what Christ endured should motivate believers to spread the Gospel, knowing the dire consequences of rejecting it.

The crucifixion of Christ is the epitome of suffering in the New Testament, showcasing how God can allow suffering for His divine purposes. It exposes the flaws of human independence, vindicates God's justice, and epitomizes divine love. While God did not orchestrate the suffering for these ends, He allowed it as part of His redemptive plan. The crucifixion and the subsequent resurrection become transformative events that teach humanity the limits of their autonomy and the need for submission to divine sovereignty. The crucifixion, therefore, stands as the ultimate object lesson in the narrative of human history, one that holds practical, theological, and existential implications for every believer.

CHAPTER 10: Finding Purpose in Pain

Understanding the Refining Nature of Suffering

The topic of suffering is a recurring theme throughout the Bible, from the trials of the Israelites to the sufferings of Paul and, ultimately, to the crucifixion of Jesus Christ. While it may be challenging to see purpose in pain, especially in moments of intense grief and despair, the Scriptures provide us with a framework for understanding suffering in a world that often feels random and chaotic.

The Fault Line of Human Independence

Before delving into the subject, it's essential to recognize that God did not design suffering as a means to produce growth, endurance, or character. The presence of suffering in the human experience serves as a stark reminder of the inherent flaw in our desire for independence from God's sovereignty. It is an object lesson that teaches humanity about the perils of life without God.

Suffering in a Fallen World

We live in a fallen world, marred by sin, where suffering is an inevitable part of the human condition. "For we know that the whole creation has been groaning together in the pains of childbirth until now" (Romans 8:22, ESV). Although God did not intend for suffering to exist, it is a consequence of the Fall, and He allows it for reasons that often transcend our understanding.

The Refining Nature of Suffering

Though God does not orchestrate suffering to make us stronger or more resilient, the experience of suffering can have a refining effect on our character and faith. We are like gold being refined—though the fire is not pleasant, it removes impurities. However, the goal of this refining is not merely personal growth but also a deeper understanding of our dependence on God.

Wisdom Through Suffering

James tells us to consider it pure joy when we face trials because the testing of faith produces perseverance (James 1:2-4). The idea is not that suffering is inherently good or divinely purposed for growth, but that in a world where suffering is inevitable, it can lead to greater wisdom and reliance on God when faced with integrity.

The Comfort of God in Suffering

Paul speaks of the "God of all comfort, who comforts us in all our affliction" (2 Corinthians 1:3-4, ESV). The comfort God provides does not negate the pain or make it part of a divine plan for personal development; rather, it helps us endure it. God's comfort serves as a testament to His grace and a call to share this comfort with others who are suffering.

Testimony and Evangelism

When God allows suffering and subsequently provides comfort and deliverance, it equips believers to testify to His goodness and mercies, thereby furthering the kingdom of God. Sharing our journey of suffering and comfort can be a powerful tool for evangelism.

Practical Implications

1. **Self-Examination**: Use periods of suffering to reflect on your life and recognize areas where independence from God has been sought, consciously or unconsciously.
2. **Prayer**: During suffering, deepening your prayer life becomes crucial, not to ask why the suffering occurs but to seek God's grace to endure it.
3. **Community**: Engage with a community of believers for mutual encouragement and sharing of comfort that each has received from God.
4. **Scriptural Insight**: Delve into the Bible for accounts and teachings on suffering, taking note of how biblical figures responded to their trials.
5. **Outreach**: Use your experience to minister to others who are going through similar trials, sharing the comfort you have received from God.

Suffering remains one of the most challenging aspects of human life, often defying explanation or justification. While the Bible does not offer a formulaic answer to the problem of suffering, it provides a perspective that places suffering within the context of a fallen world and a sovereign God. This view doesn't render suffering purposeful in itself but indicates that God, in His wisdom, allows it and can bring good from it, teaching us the profound lesson of our own limitations and the necessity of His sovereign grace.

By understanding that the purpose of our life is not found in the absence of suffering but in the presence of God, we come to recognize that suffering can serve to refine us, not by design, but by the sovereign allowance of a God who is in control even when we are not.

God's Ultimate Plan for Our Lives

Many wrestle with the daunting question of the purpose of life, especially when encountering pain and suffering. While these trials are emotionally and sometimes physically taxing, understanding God's ultimate plan for our lives can provide a framework to make sense of these difficult experiences.

God's Sovereignty and Human Limitations

God's sovereignty is a cornerstone concept in understanding His ultimate plan for our lives. While God did not design suffering as a mechanism for our growth or development, He allows it as an object lesson to humanity about the perils of life outside His will. The mere presence of suffering serves as a vivid reminder of our limitations and the consequences of our departure from God's sovereignty.

The Ultimate Goal: Knowing and Glorifying God

According to the Scriptures, the chief aim of human existence is to glorify God and enjoy Him forever. This concept transcends the idea that life's purpose is happiness, comfort, or even personal development. "So, whether you eat or drink, or whatever you do, do all to the glory of God" (1 Corinthians 10:31, ESV). In a world marred by sin and suffering, every experience can draw us closer to this ultimate purpose when seen through the lens of God's sovereignty.

The Role of Suffering in God's Ultimate Plan

While it is difficult to comprehend fully, suffering has a place in God's ultimate plan for our lives, not as a tool for our improvement but as a lesson in dependency. Suffering, in this context, becomes a reminder of our limitations and drives us towards a fuller realization of God's sovereignty.

Free Will and God's Plan

Another crucial aspect to consider is the role of free will in God's ultimate plan. While God is sovereign, He has given humans free will to make choices. Often, the suffering we encounter is the direct or indirect result of human choices, whether our own or those of others.

Yet, even in this complex interplay between divine sovereignty and human free will, God can work "all things together for good, for those who are called according to his purpose" (Romans 8:28, ESV).

The Heavenly Hope and Earthly Hope

Christian hope is dichotomous; it can be heavenly or earthly. For some, the earthly hope means a life led in righteousness, enjoying the blessings of creation and relationships while giving glory to God. For others, it's the heavenly hope—the anticipation of eternal life with God, which serves as the ultimate form of restoration and realization of God's plan.

Navigating Suffering: Practical Steps

1. **Scriptural Meditations**: Immerse yourself in the Word of God to understand His character and promises during periods of suffering.

2. **Prayer**: Open communication with God is vital. Instead of asking God to take away the suffering, pray for wisdom to understand your dependency on Him.

3. **Community Support**: The body of Christ is crucial for support, encouragement, and practical help during trying times.

4. **Surrender**: This involves letting go of our need to control outcomes and submitting to God's sovereignty, trusting that He has an ultimate plan, even if it's beyond our understanding.

5. **Testimony**: Share your experiences and the lessons you've learned about God's sovereignty with others, thereby magnifying God's glory and encouraging fellow believers.

Finding purpose in pain is not about decoding a secret message from God or striving for self-improvement. Rather, it's about realigning our perspective to recognize that God has an ultimate plan for our lives, which is to bring glory to Him. Understanding this can provide solace and perspective during times of suffering, driving us closer to God and further from the delusion that we can navigate life independently of Him.

The goal is not to escape suffering but to learn through it—how to know God more deeply, to understand our limitations, and to glorify God in every circumstance. Thus, even when we walk through the darkest valleys of life, we can do so with the confidence that God is sovereign, and His ultimate plan is for our good and His glory.

Transforming Pain into Ministry

In the journey of life, pain is often an inevitable companion. Yet, one of the most profound ways to find purpose in that pain is to channel it into ministry. While suffering wasn't designed by God for our growth or moral improvement, it serves as an object lesson teaching us about our limitations and the necessity of relying on God's sovereignty. Let's delve into how you can transform your pain into a ministry that honors God.

The Concept of Ministry in the Midst of Suffering

Ministry is not merely about preaching, teaching, or performing religious rites; it encompasses serving others in a Christ-like manner. The Apostle Paul exhorts us, "Bear one another's burdens, and so fulfill the law of Christ" (Galatians 6:2, ESV). The implication here is that by aiding others in their struggles, we're effectively doing the work of the ministry. Suffering equips us with empathy and understanding, tools vital in ministering to others.

God's Sovereignty in Ministry

It's crucial to remember that God's ultimate plan for our lives revolves around His sovereignty. Our aim in transforming pain into ministry should not be self-centered but God-centered. Pain serves to remind us that we can't live independently from God; it functions as a lesson to draw us back to His purpose for our lives.

The Power of Personal Testimony

One of the most compelling ways to minister to others is through your own story. Testimonies are compelling narratives of God's faithfulness and your own human frailty. While we must remember that suffering isn't a God-designed mechanism for growth, it nonetheless serves as a platform to talk about our dependence on God. By sharing how God's sovereignty has guided us through tough times, we extend an invitation to others to explore this divine truth.

The Ministry of Presence

Sometimes ministry doesn't involve grand gestures or articulate words but simply being there for someone. The ministry of presence reflects Jesus' own ministry to the broken-hearted and marginalized. By being present in someone's pain, we echo the reality that God is also present with us in our suffering, not as a designer but as a sovereign guide.

Building a Ministry: Practical Steps

1. **Prayer and Discernment**: Pray for guidance on how God wants you to use your pain in service to Him and others.
2. **Utilize Your Gifts**: Everyone has unique gifts given by God for the building up of the body of Christ. Use yours in areas related to your experience of pain to minister to others.
3. **Seek Accountability and Support**: Always have someone who can keep you accountable, so your ministry remains aligned with Scriptural truth.
4. **Consistency and Commitment**: Genuine ministry requires ongoing effort and commitment. Make sure you are consistent in whatever ministry you are led to.
5. **Biblical Guidance**: Always ground your ministry efforts in Scripture, which is the inspired Word of God, making it the final authority for faith and life.

Coping with Obstacles

In ministry, you will face hurdles. You may deal with criticism, burnout, or even doubt. In those moments, remember that your purpose isn't to resolve all issues or to be a savior but to serve as a conduit of God's love and sovereignty. When you encounter obstacles, revisit the essence of why you are doing what you're doing: to bring glory to God.

The journey of transforming pain into ministry is an ongoing process, one that requires submission to God's sovereignty, diligent prayer, and a willingness to serve. It allows us to step beyond the realm of our struggles into a broader arena where our pain serves as a continual reminder of our human limitations and God's limitless power.

While suffering is not a divine mechanism for personal growth, it can serve as a poignant lesson that compels us to rely on God. In the process, it enables us to minister to others more effectively, fulfilling God's ultimate plan for our lives: to know Him and to make Him known. Thus, even in the midst of suffering, we find a purpose that transcends our pain, aiming for the glory of God and the expansion of His Kingdom.

Edward D. Andrews

CHAPTER 11: The Role of the Church in Alleviating Suffering

The Biblical Mandate for Community Support

The question of how to grapple with suffering is not only an individual concern but also a collective one for the Church. As a body of believers, the Church plays a pivotal role in alleviating the pain experienced by its members. While it's important to understand that God did not design suffering to teach us lessons in character or endurance, He allows it as an object lesson demonstrating our need for His sovereignty. This chapter aims to elucidate the biblical mandate that commands the Church to act as a support system for those in distress.

The New Testament Vision of the Church

When we look at the New Testament, we find that the early Church was not just a place where people gathered to worship; it was a community. Members sold their possessions to support one another (Acts 2:45, ESV), and they met regularly for fellowship and breaking of bread (Acts 2:42, ESV). The vision for the Church is as a support system that mirrors the unity of the body of Christ, as described in 1 Corinthians 12:12-27.

The Biblical Mandate: "Bear One Another's Burdens"

The Apostle Paul explicitly lays out the Church's role in Galatians 6:2, stating, "Bear one another's burdens, and so fulfill the law of Christ" (ESV). This isn't a suggestion; it's a command that reflects the higher law of love, emphasizing the corporate responsibility to support those who are suffering. This also serves as an indirect acknowledgment of God's sovereignty, showing us how we are not designed to handle suffering independently.

Practical Ways the Church Can Support

1. **Prayer Gatherings**: Organize times of prayer specifically focused on members who are going through trials.
2. **Resource Allocation**: Utilize church funds or donations to assist those in need, perhaps by establishing a benevolent fund.
3. **Counseling Services**: Pastoral care and biblically grounded counseling can be invaluable for someone navigating suffering.
4. **Visitations**: Sometimes, being physically present can provide tremendous comfort. Organizing visitation schedules for the sick and distressed can be a practical step.
5. **Teaching and Preaching**: The pulpit must be used to address the subject of suffering and God's sovereignty, providing a theological framework for understanding one's experience.

How Community Supports Reflect God's Sovereignty

By acting as a pillar of support for those enduring hardship, the Church stands as a practical demonstration of God's sovereignty. In a world marked by suffering, the Church should be a haven where people find not the reasons for their pain, but the means to cope through divine reliance. This, in essence, is a tacit acknowledgment that God is in control, even when circumstances appear otherwise.

Potential Challenges and Solutions

1. Lack of Willingness: Sometimes, people may not want to get involved. The solution lies in fostering a culture of service and love, starting from the church leadership.

2. Resource Limitations: Smaller congregations may feel they don't have adequate resources. Here, creativity can go a long way—small gestures often make a significant impact.

3. Theological Confusion: Wrong teaching about the reasons for suffering can harm more than help. Thus, it's vital to be grounded in Scriptural truth.

While suffering serves as a reminder of the flawed nature of human independence and the necessity for divine governance, the Church has a crucial role to play in alleviating it. By being obedient to the biblical mandate of mutual support and burden-bearing, the Church not only ministers to its members but also stands as a testament to the greater theological reality of God's sovereignty.

Through deliberate acts of kindness, the sharing of resources, and providing emotional and spiritual support, the Church embodies the love of Christ in a broken world. We must remember that we aren't merely individuals striving to find peace in a chaotic world; we are part of a body, called to live in unity and to reflect the sovereignty and love of God even—and especially—in times of suffering. This calls for a collective response, a communal ethos that takes seriously the command to "rejoice with those who rejoice, weep with those who weep" (Romans 12:15, ESV). It's through this collective obedience that the Church serves as a beacon, pointing to the ultimate Sovereign who governs all.

How the Early Church Responded to Suffering

Understanding the role of the Church in alleviating suffering necessitates a historical lens, focusing on how the early Church managed this issue. The early Christians encountered diverse forms of suffering: social ostracization, economic hardships, and even life-threatening persecution. Amidst these tribulations, the early Church provided a model of how to respond to suffering within a framework that underscores God's sovereignty. While God did not design suffering for character building or endurance, it serves as an object lesson teaching us the peril of independence from His sovereignty.

The Community-Centric Model

The early Church was, at its core, a community. Believers not only shared spiritual beliefs but also material possessions to alleviate each other's sufferings. Acts 2:45 (ESV) narrates, "And they were selling their possessions and belongings and distributing the proceeds to all, as any had need." This active participation in bearing each other's burdens was not incidental but rooted in the understanding of God's sovereignty and the problematic nature of human self-reliance.

Persecution and the Early Church

One of the most vivid examples of suffering in the early Church was persecution, particularly under Roman rule. Despite the risks involved, the early Christians remained steadfast in their faith. They understood their trials within the broader context of God's sovereignty. For example, Paul and Silas sang hymns in prison (Acts 16:25, ESV), demonstrating not a masochistic acceptance of suffering but a profound acknowledgment of God's overarching governance.

The Role of Church Leadership

The early Church leadership took the responsibility of addressing and mitigating suffering seriously. James 5:14 (ESV) says, "Is anyone among you sick? Let him call for the elders of the church, and let them pray over him..." Leaders like the Apostles Peter and Paul not only provided theological explanations for suffering but also practical steps for community support. They acknowledged suffering as an object lesson, steering people away from the pitfall of self-reliance and towards the sovereignty of God.

Financial and Material Support

The early Church also extended financial help to fellow congregations that were struggling. For instance, Paul collected contributions for the Jerusalem church from the Gentile churches he visited (1 Corinthians 16:1–4, ESV). This practice wasn't merely altruistic; it reflected a fundamental theological belief in God's sovereignty and the understanding that human efforts are insufficient without divine governance.

Emotional and Spiritual Support

The Epistles are filled with examples of emotional and spiritual support extended to suffering believers. Letters often included prayers, affirmations, and encouragement to persevere, recognizing that only through acknowledging God's sovereignty could one navigate the maze of human suffering effectively.

Pastoral Care and Counseling

While the concept of professional counseling did not exist in the early Church, pastoral care was often provided to help members navigate their struggles. This included Scriptural guidance, prayers, and sometimes even deliverance from life-threatening situations through divine intervention.

Lessons for Today

The early Church serves as a prototype for how contemporary churches should approach suffering among its members. The focus should be on:

1. **Community Sharing**: Create a culture of generosity where needs are met willingly.
2. **Theological Clarity**: Consistently teach that suffering serves as an object lesson from God, driving us towards His sovereignty.

3. **Emotional Support**: Facilitate support groups, prayer chains, and other platforms for emotional healing.
4. **Spiritual Oversight**: Church leaders should be well-equipped to offer pastoral care, always pointing towards the ultimate sovereignty of God.

The early Church's approach to alleviating suffering was deeply rooted in a theological understanding of God's sovereignty and human insufficiency. In fulfilling its role as a supportive community, the Church functioned not only as a haven for its members but also as a living, breathing example of the object lesson that God intends for humanity to learn from suffering. We must remember that, while we experience suffering, we are part of a community founded on the understanding of God's ultimate governance. The Church, then as now, serves to reaffirm God's sovereignty in our lives, reminding us that we cannot navigate the complexities of existence in our strength. This is the crux of the object lesson we are living through, and it's a lesson the Church must continue to teach.

Modern-Day Applications for Churches

In examining the role of the modern Church in alleviating suffering, it is crucial to consider the historical roots of how the early Church responded to such issues. Although the cultural and societal dynamics have evolved, the underlying theological principles rooted in God's sovereignty remain the same. The modern Church should be a beacon, reflecting God's governance and illustrating to society that suffering is an object lesson teaching the importance of relying on God's sovereignty rather than human effort.

Theological Foundation

Before diving into practical applications, it is essential to reiterate the theological cornerstone that should guide all activities: God's sovereignty. God didn't design suffering to foster growth, endurance, or character but allows it to demonstrate the inherent flaw in human independence from His sovereignty. The objective is to realign our priorities and help us recognize that, apart from God, we cannot function effectively.

Practical Application 1: Community Programs

Just as the early Church had a community-centric model, the modern Church should be actively engaged in community outreach programs. Whether it is food banks, health clinics, or shelters for the homeless, these initiatives should be rooted in the desire to embody God's love and sovereignty in a world entrapped by the illusion of self-sufficiency.

Practical Application 2: Emotional and Psychological Support

Modern churches have the resources to offer professional counseling services, often integrating biblical principles. However, the key is to ensure that the counseling is not just a secular exercise but one that centers on the sovereignty of God as the ultimate solution to human suffering.

Practical Application 3: Financial Assistance

Today's churches often have more extensive financial resources than their early counterparts. Establishing funds to aid those in need within the community and also extend help internationally can be a powerful testimony to the Church's commitment to embodying God's sovereignty.

Practical Application 4: Spiritual Development Programs

Suffering often leads people to question their faith. The Church should offer structured Bible studies, workshops, and retreats that focus on the issue of suffering within the framework of God's sovereignty. Participants should come away understanding that their trials are an object lesson designed by God to reveal the folly of human independence.

Practical Application 5: Training for Church Leadership

Church leaders should be well-equipped to deal with issues related to suffering. Specialized training programs should be developed to equip them with the skills to provide theological, emotional, and practical support to those undergoing various forms of suffering.

Practical Application 6: Leveraging Technology

With the advent of technology, the Church can extend its reach far beyond its physical boundaries. Webinars, online courses, and social media platforms should be utilized to teach biblical perspectives on suffering, emphasizing the importance of recognizing God's sovereignty.

Practical Application 7: Partnership with Other Organizations

No church is an island. Collaborating with other Christian organizations and even non-religious bodies committed to alleviating suffering can multiply the Church's impact. However, the Church should ensure that these collaborations do not dilute its core theological stance regarding God's sovereignty.

Practical Application 8: A Culture of Openness

The Church should foster a culture where individuals feel comfortable sharing their struggles without fear of judgment. This environment of openness can be instrumental in helping people see their trials as an object lesson from God rather than pointless suffering.

The role of the modern Church in alleviating suffering is multi-faceted and complex, influenced by various societal, cultural, and technological factors. However, the underlying principle that should guide all these activities is the sovereignty of God. The Church serves as a living example of the object lesson that suffering offers, highlighting the folly of human independence from God's rule. By focusing on practical applications that embody this theological understanding, the Church can be a powerful agent for change, drawing people closer to the realization of God's ultimate sovereignty in their lives. This realization is not merely theoretical; it has real, tangible implications for how we, as a faith community, respond to the suffering around us.

CHAPTER 12: Understanding Hell: Eternal Torment or Eternal Destruction?

Scriptural Insights into the Nature of Hell

A topic of profound gravity in Christian theology is the nature of Hell. It has been the subject of numerous debates, speculations, and misconceptions. To navigate through these complexities, it is essential to rely solely on what Scripture reveals. The Bible does not support the view of Hell as a place of eternal torment but describes it as the common grave of humankind, a state of eternal destruction.

Theological Foundation

As we explore this topic, the overarching theological foundation should be the sovereignty of God. Suffering, sin, and ultimately, Hell, serve as an object lesson that teaches humanity about the necessity of abiding by God's sovereign will and the severe consequences of failing to do so.

Hades: The Common Grave

Hades, translated from the Greek word "ἄδης" (hadēs), corresponds to the Hebrew term "Sheol." It occurs in multiple passages, including Matthew 11:23, Luke 16:23, and Acts 2:27. Far from being a place of eternal torment, Hades is described as a place where the dead are "conscious of nothing" and are in a state of waiting for a resurrection (John 5:28-29; Acts 24:15). This matches the Old Testament's depiction of Sheol, which is similarly not a place of punishment but a resting place for both the righteous and the unrighteous. It is the wages of sin, as the Apostle Paul stated in Romans 6:23, "For the wages of sin is death, but the free gift of God is eternal life in Christ Jesus our Lord."

Gehenna: Symbol of Eternal Destruction

Gehenna originates from the Valley of Hinnom, known for its heinous practices, including child sacrifices. This valley was later used as a waste incinerator where rubbish and even dead bodies were burned. In the New Testament, Gehenna serves as a symbolic representation of eternal destruction or the "second death," not eternal torment. It appears in several passages such as Matthew 5:22 and Mark 9:43-48, underscoring the irreversible nature of this destruction.

Sheol: Awaiting Resurrection

Sheol is the Hebrew term that corresponds to the Greek term "Hades." Like Hades, Sheol is also the common grave where the dead await resurrection (John 5:28-29; Acts 24:15). In the Old Testament, Sheol appears in places like Genesis 37:35 and Psalm 16:10. It, too, is not a place of torment but rather a state of unconsciousness until the day of judgment.

Tartarus: Condition of the Fallen Angels

Tartarus is unique in that it is not directly related to human destiny but is associated with the fallen angels who rebelled against God. These beings were stripped of specific powers and were placed in a weakened condition. It is a state or condition rather than a location, as described in 2 Peter 2:4. This restriction serves as a divine act of justice and a warning to the created beings about the severe consequences of rebellion.

Reconciling with the Sovereignty of God

Understanding Hell within this framework aligns with the principle that God did not create suffering to build character or endurance, but rather to serve as an object lesson. Hell stands as a testament to what happens when beings choose to live independently of God's sovereign will. This is not arbitrary cruelty but divine justice, an eternal reminder of the choices made in temporal life and the irrevocable consequences that follow.

The Bible's depiction of Hell as a state of eternal destruction rather than a place of eternal torment is critical for us to understand the nature of divine justice and the gravity of sin. God's sovereignty is not designed to make us suffer endlessly but to teach us that our independent ways lead to destruction. Therefore, Hell should not be seen as contrary to God's love or fairness, but as a just consequence and an eternal object lesson for creation. The grave warnings about Hell serve as a sobering call to align our lives with the sovereign God, understanding that to do otherwise leads not to eternal torment but to eternal destruction.

Debunking Common Misconceptions

The concept of Hell has long been a subject of misunderstanding and misconception in both the Christian community and the broader culture. Many have pictured Hell as a place of unending, eternal torment, where souls are condemned to suffer ceaselessly. This image has been perpetuated by various sources, ranging from theological treatises to popular media. However, a careful, literal examination of Scripture reveals a different reality.

The Biblical Terms for Hell and Their Meanings

1. **Hades**: The term "Hades" appears in the New Testament (e.g., Matt. 11:23; Acts 2:31) and corresponds to the Hebrew term "Sheol" in the Old Testament. Far from being a place of eternal torment, Hades is described as the common grave of humankind, where individuals are conscious of nothing and await resurrection (John 5:28-29; Acts 24:15).

2. **Gehenna**: This term occurs twelve times in the New Testament and refers to the Valley of Hinnom, a physical location southwest of Jerusalem. In the past, this valley was the site of horrendous acts, including idolatrous practices. Jesus used "Gehenna" to symbolize eternal destruction or annihilation, commonly known as the "second death" (Rev. 20:14).

3. **Sheol**: This term appears in the Old Testament and is rendered as "Hades" in the Greek Septuagint. Like Hades, Sheol is a place where the dead await resurrection, without consciousness or torment (Gen. 37:35; Psa. 16:10).

4. **Tartarus**: This term is unique and refers not to a place but to a condition. Specifically, it describes the restrained state of fallen angels who disobeyed God (2 Pet. 2:4).

Misconceptions About Hell

1. **Eternal Torment**: The most widespread misconception is that Hell is a place of eternal torment. This image often stems from a misreading or traditional interpretation of texts like Revelation 20:10. However, these texts are not speaking about human souls but refer to entities like the Devil, the Beast, and the False Prophet.

2. **Universalism**: Another misconception is the belief that all individuals will ultimately be saved. This contradicts Jesus' own words that the path to destruction is broad, while the path to life is narrow (Matt. 7:13-14).

3. **Eternal Security**: The idea that once a person is saved, they are always saved, is not supported by Scripture. Texts like Hebrews 6:4-6 and 2 Peter 2:20-22 make it clear that it's possible to fall away from the faith.

4. **Physical Torture**: Imagery of fire and brimstone has often been misunderstood as indicating physical torture. However, these are symbols of complete destruction and purification, not eternal suffering.

The Sovereignty of God in Allowing Suffering

While discussing Hell, it's vital to understand that God's allowing of suffering is not for the purpose of character development or punishment per se. Rather, God has allowed suffering to occur as an object lesson in the importance of His sovereignty. Mankind, in its state of rebellion and sin, experiences the consequences of living independently from God. Thus, the ultimate consequence, Hell, serves as a final, sobering object lesson.

A correct understanding of Hell—based on a literal, historical-grammatical interpretation of Scripture—reveals it as a place of eternal destruction, not eternal torment. This aligns with the Biblical affirmations about the nature of God as just, loving, and sovereign. Such a view avoids the pitfalls of traditional misconceptions, offering a more accurate, Scripturally-grounded understanding. This Scriptural clarity also provides profound implications for Christian living and evangelism, emphasizing the weight of the choices we make in this life and their eternal consequences.

The Role of Judgment and Mercy

The notion of Hell has been a topic of great contention, and misunderstandings about its nature abound. Traditional views often present Hell as a place of unending torment and anguish. However, a thorough examination of Scripture, employing an objective Historical-Grammatical method, reveals that Hell is not a place of eternal torment but rather the ultimate expression of divine judgment: eternal destruction. This understanding aligns more closely with the character of a just and merciful God. In this chapter, we will explore the nature of Hell through the various terms used in Scripture: Hades, Sheol, Gehenna, and Tartarus, and we will examine how these concepts relate to divine judgment and mercy.

Hades: A Waiting Place for the Dead

Hades is often translated from the Greek word ᾅδης (hadēs), and its essential meaning is a place where the dead await resurrection. Hades is the common grave of mankind, a place of unconsciousness where the dead await the resurrection (John 5:28-29; Acts 24:15). This aligns with the warning given to Adam that disobedience would result in death (Gen. 2:17). The apostle Paul confirms that the "wages of sin is death" (Rom. 6:23) and not eternal torment. Paul further indicates that those who do not know God and do not obey the gospel will face "eternal destruction" (2 Thessalonians 1:8-9).

Gehenna: The Second Death

Gehenna, or γέεννα (geenna), is another term used to depict Hell in the New Testament. The term originates from the Valley of Hinnom, which was a literal place near Jerusalem where trash and dead bodies were incinerated. Jesus and his disciples used Gehenna to symbolize eternal destruction, the "second death" where there is no hope of resurrection (Rev. 20:14-15).

Sheol: The Grave

In the Old Testament, Sheol serves a similar function to Hades in the New Testament. It's a place where the dead, both righteous and unrighteous, await resurrection, conscious of nothing (Ecclesiastes 9:5). They are not in a state of torment but rather in a state similar to sleep, from which they can be awakened through resurrection (John 5:28-29; Acts 24:15).

Tartarus: The Condition of the Fallen Angels

Tartarus is different from the aforementioned terms, in that it describes a condition rather than a place. Tartarus is the state in which certain fallen angels exist after being stripped of their powers. This is a form of divine judgment against their rebellion and is not applicable to human beings (2 Peter 2:4).

The Role of Judgment and Mercy

The concept of Hell as eternal destruction rather than eternal torment aligns more closely with God's nature as a just and merciful deity. Justice is served in that the wages of sin are death, not unending torment (Rom. 6:23). Moreover, mercy is exemplified through the provision of Jesus Christ, who offers eternal life to all who will believe and obey him (John 3:16; Hebrews 5:9).

God's sovereignty is paramount, and humanity has been undergoing an object lesson to grasp the consequences of independence from Him. This lesson has not been intended to build character or endurance, but rather to highlight our innate need for God's rulership. Hell, or eternal destruction, serves as the ultimate outcome for those who reject this lesson and continue to live independently of God's sovereignty.

Scriptural evidence, when carefully and conservatively interpreted, supports the understanding of Hell as eternal destruction rather than a place of everlasting torment. This fits within the framework of a God who is both just and merciful. Judgment is carried out, but mercy is available to all who will accept it. By grasping this biblical perspective, we gain a more coherent and theologically sound understanding of divine judgment and mercy.

CHAPTER 13: Coping Mechanisms: Healthy vs. Unhealthy

Scriptural Guidance on Coping Strategies

Life is fraught with challenges, trials, and suffering. The question is not whether we will face these obstacles, but how we cope with them when they arise. As believers, we look to Scripture for guidance in times of hardship. However, not all coping mechanisms are created equal. Some are healthy and Scripturally-grounded, while others can lead to spiritual, emotional, and physical decline. This chapter aims to differentiate between healthy and unhealthy coping mechanisms, providing Scriptural guidance on effective ways to deal with life's difficulties.

Healthy Coping Mechanisms

1. **Prayer and Meditation**: One of the most powerful coping mechanisms offered in the Scripture is prayer. Philippians 4:6-7 urges us to "not be anxious about anything, but in everything by prayer and supplication with thanksgiving let your requests be made known to God." Prayer offers us a channel to unload our concerns and anxieties onto a loving God, who is fully in control.

2. **Word of God**: Immersing ourselves in Scripture provides not only comfort but also guidance. Hebrews 4:12 tells us that the Word of God is "living and active, sharper than any two-edged sword." It gives us insights into God's character, promises, and His plan for humanity.

3. **Community Support**: The church plays a pivotal role in coping with life's challenges. James 5:16 exhorts us to "confess your sins to one another and pray for one another, that you may be healed." This communal aspect of coping is crucial as it surrounds us with fellow believers who can offer support, prayer, and advice.

4. **Physical Health**: The apostle Paul highlights that our bodies are "temples of the Holy Spirit" (1 Corinthians 6:19). Maintaining physical health through exercise and proper nutrition can greatly aid in coping with stress and challenges.

5. **Purposeful Activity**: Engaging in activities that align with God's purpose can offer a great sense of accomplishment and peace. Paul instructs us to work "as for the Lord" (Colossians 3:23), emphasizing that even in our earthly endeavors, we are serving a higher purpose.

6. **Spiritual Discernment**: The ability to distinguish between what is from God and what is not is crucial. 1 John 4:1 advises us to "test the spirits to see whether they are from God." Discernment keeps us grounded in truth and prevents us from adopting ungodly coping mechanisms.

Unhealthy Coping Mechanisms

1. **Substance Abuse**: Resorting to alcohol, drugs, or any form of substance to escape problems is contrary to Scripture. Proverbs 20:1 warns that "wine is a mocker, strong drink is raging: and whosoever is deceived thereby is not wise."

2. **Excessive Escapism**: While recreation has its place, excessive escapism through entertainment, video games, or other activities leads to a neglect of responsibilities and could cause more harm than good.

3. **Vindictiveness**: An eye for an eye is not a healthy coping mechanism. Romans 12:19 cautions against revenge, encouraging us to leave room for God's wrath.

4. **Isolation**: Withdrawing from community support leaves one vulnerable to spiritual attacks. Hebrews 10:25 exhorts us not to neglect meeting together, emphasizing the importance of communal worship and support.
5. **False Doctrine**: Relying on teachings that are not grounded in Scripture for comfort can lead to eternal consequences. 2 Timothy 4:3 warns against accumulating teachers that suit one's own passions rather than adhering to sound doctrine.

Scriptural Perspectives on Coping with Suffering

It's important to recognize that while God did not design suffering to foster growth or character, He has allowed it as an object lesson to demonstrate humanity's inherent flaws and the dangers of independence from His sovereignty. The key to coping lies not in escaping suffering but in navigating it through Scriptural means, ever mindful of God's sovereignty and our need for Him.

In this life, suffering is inevitable, but how we choose to cope makes a significant difference. Scripture offers invaluable wisdom and practical strategies for coping with life's challenges in a manner that honors God. Utilizing healthy coping mechanisms that align with God's Word not only improves our well-being but deepens our relationship with Him. On the flip side, relying on unhealthy coping mechanisms distances us from God and may lead to further suffering. As we navigate the trials of life, let us remember that the ultimate coping mechanism is a life grounded in Scripture, ever cognizant of God's sovereign hand in all things.

Identifying and Avoiding Unbiblical Coping Mechanisms

Life's difficulties are inescapable. However, how we respond to life's adversities can either lead us to spiritual growth or downfall. While the previous chapter focused on healthy, Scripturally-grounded coping mechanisms, this chapter is dedicated to identifying and avoiding unbiblical coping strategies. It is critical for believers to be discerning, so as not to inadvertently adopt mechanisms that are at odds with the Scriptures.

Identifying Unbiblical Coping Mechanisms

1. **Reliance on Human Wisdom**: The danger here lies in leaning on one's own understanding or the worldly perspectives of others, disregarding the wisdom from above. Proverbs 3:5-7 admonishes us to "Trust in the Lord with all your heart, and do not lean on your own understanding."

2. **Emotional Overindulgence**: Whether it's bouts of anger, self-pity, or unfounded fears, giving in to emotions without Scriptural restraint can lead us astray. Ephesians 4:26 warns, "Be angry and do not sin; do not let the sun go down on your anger."

3. **Unscriptural Rituals**: Engaging in rituals or traditions that are not grounded in Scripture, in the belief that they will provide relief, is perilous. Mark 7:7-8 warns against holding to the "traditions of men" rather than the commandments of God.

4. **Prosperity Theology**: The false teaching that God's blessings are predominantly materialistic and that suffering can be escaped through sufficient faith is a dangerous coping mechanism. 1 Timothy 6:9 cautions against those who desire to be rich and fall into temptation.

5. **Moral Relativism**: Abandoning moral absolutes from Scripture to cope with difficulties is a slippery slope. Isaiah 5:20 warns against calling evil good and good evil.

6. **Selective Scriptural Application**: Using certain Scriptures out of context to justify behaviors or attitudes is misleading. 2 Timothy 2:15 encourages us to rightly handle the Word of truth.

Avoiding Unbiblical Coping Mechanisms

1. **Ground Yourself in the Word**: A robust understanding of Scripture provides a safeguard against unbiblical coping mechanisms. Psalm 119:11 encourages us to store up God's Word in our hearts that we might not sin against Him.

2. **Community Accountability**: Surrounding ourselves with godly influences can act as a buffer against adopting unbiblical coping strategies. Galatians 6:1 speaks of restoring a brother caught in transgression in a spirit of gentleness.

3. **Prayer and Spiritual Discernment**: Continual dialogue with God, along with the discernment He provides, protects us from wrong choices. James 1:5 promises wisdom to those who ask God.

4. **Consult Godly Counsel**: Seeking advice from those who are well-versed in Scripture can offer a necessary second opinion. Proverbs 11:14 speaks of safety in an abundance of counselors.

The Role of Suffering in Coping

It's essential to remember that God has allowed suffering for specific reasons. While He did not create suffering for the growth of character, endurance, or any virtue, He permits it to showcase the devastating consequences of human autonomy apart from His divine guidance. This perspective should profoundly influence how we cope, steering us away from solutions that suggest we can manage or eliminate suffering through our efforts or 'positive thinking.'

Navigating life's hardships requires more than just human resilience; it requires a God-centered approach to coping. Adopting unbiblical coping mechanisms can result in not just temporal but eternal setbacks. Therefore, it's of paramount importance that believers remain vigilant, using the lens of Scripture to identify and avoid unbiblical methods of coping. This not only preserves our spiritual well-being but also deepens our understanding of our reliance on God's sovereignty, particularly in times of suffering.

When we understand that our struggles serve as object lessons pointing us back to the necessity of God's sovereignty, our coping mechanisms will naturally align with the wisdom laid out in the Scriptures. This alignment brings us into a fuller and more harmonious relationship with God, solidifying our reliance on His sovereign will over our lives.

Turning to Scripture and Prayer for Comfort

In the Christian journey, there will be trials and tribulations that each believer faces. These hardships often raise the question: How should a Christian cope? While the world offers various coping mechanisms, not all are aligned with the principles set forth in the Scriptures. This chapter focuses on turning to Scripture and prayer as foundational elements for coping in a manner that glorifies God and aligns with His will.

The Vital Role of Scripture in Coping

1. **A Source of Eternal Truth**: Scripture provides us with unchanging truths that serve as an anchor in times of trouble. As Hebrews 4:12 states, "For the word of God is living and active, sharper than any two-edged sword."

2. **Spiritual Guidance**: The Bible offers wisdom that supersedes human understanding, equipping us to navigate life's challenges. Psalm 119:105 declares, "Your word is a lamp to my feet and a light to my path."

3. **Character Formation**: While God does not inflict suffering to cultivate virtues in us, understanding the Biblical perspective on suffering can lead us to spiritual maturity. James 1:22 reminds us to be "doers of the word, and not hearers only."

4. **Promise of Deliverance**: The Bible is filled with promises of God's intervention and deliverance for those who trust in Him.

Romans 8:28 affirms, "And we know that for those who love God all things work together for good."

5. **Emotional and Mental Relief**: Reflecting on Scriptural truths can bring mental and emotional peace, as emphasized in Philippians 4:8, which urges us to think on things that are noble and pure.

The Significance of Prayer in Coping

1. **Direct Communication with God**: Prayer enables us to have an intimate conversation with God, who can handle our fears, anxieties, and needs. Philippians 4:6 advises, "Do not be anxious about anything, but in everything by prayer and supplication with thanksgiving let your requests be made known to God."
2. **Spiritual Warfare**: Prayer is a weapon against the schemes of the enemy, equipping us to stand firm in faith. Ephesians 6:18 exhorts us to "pray at all times in the Spirit, with all prayer and supplication."
3. **Community Intercession**: Prayer provides a platform for collective support within the body of Christ, as emphasized in James 5:16, "Therefore, confess your sins to one another and pray for one another, that you may be healed."
4. **Alignment with God's Will**: Prayer helps us align our will with God's, thereby ensuring that we are walking in obedience to Him. Jesus' prayer in the Garden of Gethsemane, "Not my will, but yours, be done," serves as a powerful example (Luke 22:42).

Connecting Scripture and Prayer for Effective Coping

Combining the study of Scripture with prayer can result in a more profound understanding of God's will, as both practices feed off each other. Reading Scripture can inspire prayer topics, while prayer opens our hearts to receive the wisdom contained in God's Word. They act synergistically to guide us in walking faithfully, even in the face of suffering and challenges.

Addressing the Role of Suffering

It is crucial to note that suffering, while not designed by God for growth or character building, serves as an object lesson about the dire consequences of human independence from God's sovereignty. Turning to Scripture and prayer during times of hardship can remind us of our total dependence on Him and serve as a course correction towards His divine will.

Scripture and prayer are indispensable tools for a Christian navigating life's trials. They offer not just solace but real, tangible ways to cope that align with the nature and will of God. This alignment is crucial, especially when we consider that suffering serves to highlight the gravity of human autonomy apart from God.

By consistently turning to Scripture and prayer, we acknowledge our limitations and express our trust in God's sovereign plan. We gain not only comfort but also the wisdom and strength to face whatever challenges come our way. This approach not only honors God but also fortifies us against the difficulties we encounter, leading us to a life that is more resilient, spiritually grounded, and aligned with the divine plan that God has set forth.

CHAPTER 14: The Hope of Resurrection and Eternal Life

The Christian Belief in the Resurrection of the Dead

One of the most compelling aspects of Christian doctrine is the belief in the resurrection of the dead and eternal life. This hope sets Christianity apart from other worldviews and religious systems. Yet, what does Scripture teach about the resurrection, and how does this relate to our understanding of eternal life, especially in the face of suffering and the limitations of our mortal existence?

The Resurrection of Jesus Christ: The Cornerstone of Our Faith

Before we delve into the Christian's hope, we must first acknowledge that the resurrection of Jesus Christ serves as the bedrock of this belief. As stated in 1 Corinthians 15:17, "If Christ has not been raised, your faith is futile; you are still in your sins." The resurrection of Jesus not only validates His divinity but also confirms the future resurrection of believers.

The Two-Fold Hope: Heavenly and Earthly Existence

Scripture seems to offer two distinct hopes for humanity: a heavenly hope and an earthly hope.

1. **Heavenly Hope:** Those with a heavenly hope appear to be a limited number, chosen to reign with Christ. These individuals will be transformed, receiving glorified bodies, and will have roles as kings, priests, and judges. Scripture suggests that they will either rule on the earth or over the earth from heaven (Revelation 20:6; 2 Timothy 2:12).

2. **Earthly Hope**: The earthly hope centers on the belief that God created the earth to be inhabited by perfect humans living in harmony with His creation (Genesis 1:28). These individuals will live forever on a renewed, paradise earth, fulfilling God's original purpose (Isaiah 45:18).

The Resurrection of the Dead: A Biblical Overview

The doctrine of the resurrection of the dead is not confined to the New Testament but finds its roots in the Old Testament as well (Daniel 12:2). In the New Testament, passages like 1 Corinthians 15 detail the nature and significance of the resurrection.

1. **A Physical Resurrection**: Contrary to some belief systems that imagine an ethereal existence, the Christian hope is tied to bodily resurrection (1 Corinthians 15:42-44).
2. **Victory Over Death**: The resurrection negates the sting of death, providing hope that life has meaning beyond our mortal limitations (1 Corinthians 15:54-57).
3. **Judgment and Reward**: The resurrection is followed by a judgment where deeds are assessed, and eternal destinies determined (2 Corinthians 5:10).

Resurrection and Suffering

The doctrine of the resurrection provides comfort and perspective in times of suffering. It serves as a reminder that the trials of this life are temporary. While God has allowed suffering to serve as an object lesson about the importance of His sovereignty, He has also provided a way out through the hope of resurrection and eternal life.

The New Heavens and the New Earth

The hope of a new creation is not an afterthought but aligns with God's original purpose for humanity and the universe. The new heavens and the new earth will be characterized by God's complete rule and the realization of His redemptive plan (Revelation 21:3). This renewed creation confirms that God's goals for humans involve a bodily existence in a perfected earth, not an ethereal and disembodied existence. It signifies the full realization of the spiritual within a perfected creation.

The Christian belief in the resurrection of the dead and eternal life serves as a bedrock of hope and comfort. It provides an eternal perspective that helps us navigate the trials and tribulations of life. As we continue to live in a world where suffering is a reality, albeit one that serves as an object lesson on the inherent flaws of human independence from God's sovereignty, the doctrine of the resurrection stands as a beacon of hope. It promises not only a future transformation for believers but also the fulfilment of God's ultimate redemptive plan for the universe and humanity.

This hope is grounded in the reality that God created the earth to be inhabited and that His redemptive plan, made possible through Jesus Christ, will culminate in a renewed creation where God's rule is complete. Whether we are part of those with a heavenly hope, destined to rule with Christ, or those with an earthly hope, looking forward to life on a renewed earth, the promise remains steadfast: our hope in Christ is not in vain, but it is the assurance of glory, honor, and immortality in the presence of our sovereign God.

The Assurance of a New Heaven and New Earth

In the Christian worldview, the hope of resurrection and eternal life goes beyond merely escaping the torments of an imperfect world. It encompasses the marvelous prospect of living in a new heaven and a new earth, specifically designed by God to fulfill His eternal purpose. This chapter aims to delve deeper into the Scriptural assurance of this glorious future, a topic that serves as a powerful antidote to the suffering and challenges we face in the present world.

The Biblical Basis for a New Creation

The Bible offers vivid descriptions of a new heaven and a new earth. In Revelation 21:1, we read, "Then I saw a new heaven and a new earth, for the first heaven and the first earth had passed away, and the sea was no more." This is not just an improved version of our current world but a complete renewal.

God's Original Intent for Creation

God's purpose has always been to create a world filled with perfect humans who have dominion over the animals and live under His sovereignty (Genesis 1:28; 2:8, 15). This intent was never thwarted by human sin, as evidenced by His redemptive plan through Jesus Christ. The promise of a new heaven and a new earth is consistent with this original intention. Humans will not float in some ethereal realm but live in bodily form in a perfected earth (Isaiah 45:18).

The Spiritual and the Material: Harmoniously Intertwined

Contrary to some dualistic perspectives that consider the material world as unimportant or evil, the Christian view holds that the spiritual and the material are interrelated. The scene of the beatific vision, or the ultimate direct self-communication of God to the individual, is not an intangible heaven but a renewed earth where God's complete rule is manifested (Revelation 21:3).

A Home for the Redeemed: Heavenly Hope vs. Earthly Hope

Scripture suggests two types of hope for the redeemed:
1. **Heavenly Hope**: A limited number of humans are chosen for a heavenly life to rule with Christ as kings, priests, and judges. They will have a direct role in the administration of God's kingdom, either on earth or from heaven (Revelation 20:4-6).

2. **Earthly Hope**: The majority will inherit eternal life on a restored earth, free from sin, suffering, and death, living in perfect harmony with God's creation (Isaiah 11:6-9).

Assurance Amidst Suffering

The suffering that we witness and experience in our present world has not been designed by God but allowed to demonstrate the inherent flaw of human independence from His sovereignty. The assurance of a new heaven and a new earth serves as a powerful coping mechanism in such a context. It provides the perspective that the present state of the world is temporary and will give way to a perfect reality where God's sovereignty is unchallenged.

The Nature of the New Creation

1. **No More Suffering**: "He will wipe away every tear from their eyes, and death shall be no more, neither shall there be mourning, nor crying, nor pain anymore" (Revelation 21:4).
2. **Presence of God**: One of the most compelling aspects of the new creation is the dwelling of God with men (Revelation 21:3).
3. **Restoration and Renewal**: The new creation is not an annihilation of the old but its transformation and renewal. This aligns with God's initial purpose for creation (Romans 8:21).

Practical Implications for the Believer

1. **Hope**: The certainty of a new creation infuses hope into our lives, empowering us to persevere through trials.
2. **Purpose**: It provides a sense of purpose, directing our actions towards what is eternal rather than transitory.
3. **Assurance**: It offers a robust assurance that our labor in the Lord is not in vain but contributes to an eternal legacy (1 Corinthians 15:58).

The promise of a new heaven and a new earth, where righteousness dwells and where God's sovereignty is complete, is among the most comforting doctrines in Scripture. This future reality does not negate the hardships we face but provides the right perspective to view them. God has allowed mankind to learn through the trials and challenges of this world, but His ultimate plan is to usher us into a realm where His original purpose for creation is fulfilled in its entirety. Whether we hold a heavenly or an earthly hope, this assurance serves as a foundational pillar, influencing how we live today and shaping our expectations for the future.

Living in the 'Now' with Eternal Perspectives

The hope of resurrection and eternal life can drastically reshape how we approach life today. Often, Christians may find themselves in a tension between living for the present moment and preparing for an eternal future. This chapter explores how to harmonize these seemingly divergent focuses by cultivating an eternal perspective while engaging responsibly with the present world.

The Paradox of the 'Now' and 'Not Yet'

Scripture teaches that believers are already in a saved state ("now") but have not yet fully experienced the consummation of this salvation ("not yet"). This paradoxical existence creates a dynamic tension: we are to live as though Jesus is returning tomorrow while planning as if His return may not happen for many years.

Living as Though Jesus is Returning Tomorrow

When we live with the expectation that Jesus might return imminently, several practical and spiritual benefits manifest:

1. **Prioritization of Righteousness**: The immediacy of Christ's potential return motivates believers to seek a life of righteousness, reflecting Paul's exhortation in Romans 13:14,

"But put on the Lord Jesus Christ, and make no provision for the flesh, to gratify its desires."

2. **Vigilance in Faith**: Anticipating His return heightens our spiritual alertness, a vigilance that Jesus Himself commends (Matthew 24:42).

3. **Focus on Eternal Values**: It helps to shift our priorities towards eternal values rather than worldly ones, as emphasized by Colossians 3:2, "Set your minds on things that are above, not on things that are on earth."

Planning as Though Jesus is Returning 50 Years from Now

While the Bible encourages us to be prepared for Christ's imminent return, it also provides wisdom for long-term planning:

1. **Stewardship of Resources**: Financial planning, buying a house, or pursuing a career are not inherently secular activities but can be acts of stewardship (Matthew 25:14-30).

2. **Engagement with the World**: Christians are not called to isolate themselves but to engage with the world in a godly manner (1 Corinthians 5:9-10).

3. **Commitment to Relationships**: Building and maintaining relationships, whether familial or communal, is part of long-term planning that is highly valued in Scripture (Ephesians 5:21-6:4).

Balancing the 'Now' and 'Not Yet'

To resolve the tension between living for today and planning for the future, consider the following principles:

1. **Commit All Plans to God**: Regardless of the time frame, commit all your plans to God for His guidance and approval (Proverbs 16:3).

2. **Maintain an Eternal Perspective**: While it is wise to plan, remember that all plans are provisional and must yield to God's ultimate will (James 4:13-15).

3. **Exercise Wisdom in All Things**: Apply Scriptural wisdom in every decision-making process, understanding that wisdom does not contradict but complements faith (Proverbs 3:5-6).

Living Amidst Suffering

In a world filled with challenges and trials, we can be assured that the sufferings are not divinely designed but allowed by God to reveal the folly of human independence from His sovereignty. This awareness, however, should not lead us into fatalism or despair but into a deeper realization of our need for God's guiding hand.

Eternal Perspectives as a Coping Mechanism

The certainty of eternal life and the transformation of the heavens and earth serve as powerful coping mechanisms. The assurance of a future where God's rule is unopposed provides the perspective needed to navigate the struggles of the present world.

Practical Implications

1. **Be Diligent but Not Anxious**: Work diligently in your callings but do not be overly anxious, for God is in control (Philippians 4:6-7).

2. **Balance Temporal and Eternal**: Strive for a balanced life that gives due attention to both temporal responsibilities and eternal priorities (Matthew 6:33).

3. **Cultivate a Lifestyle of Worship**: Live each day as an offering to God, which is your spiritual worship (Romans 12:1).

The Christian hope of resurrection and eternal life offers a balanced perspective for living in the 'now.' Whether the Lord returns tomorrow or many years from now, our role remains the same: to live righteously, plan wisely, and maintain an eternal perspective. Such a mindset transforms every aspect of our lives, from how we manage our daily activities to how we cope with sufferings, reinforcing our confidence in the glorious future that God has promised. Thus, we find true purpose and meaning, understanding that we are but sojourners passing through, with our true citizenship in heaven (Philippians 3:20).

CHAPTER 15: Conclusion: Where Do We Go from Here?

Drawing Near to God in Times of Suffering

The Journey Thus Far

As we conclude this exploration of Scripture's insights into the human condition, various forms of suffering, and coping mechanisms, we must acknowledge that the journey is far from over. The principles and teachings we've discussed are not mere academic exercises; they are life-altering truths that should inform our day-to-day living and decisions. But where do we go from here?

The Reality of Suffering

It's essential to reiterate that suffering, while not designed by God, is an inevitable part of the human experience. We are not abandoned to navigate this perilous terrain alone; God is with us, providing wisdom, strength, and ultimately a hope that extends beyond this life. Suffering serves to emphasize the inherent dangers of human independence from God's sovereignty, calling us to draw near to Him as the ultimate source of hope and stability.

Spiritual Resilience

In times of suffering, one's faith is both tested and strengthened. James 1:2-4 says, "Count it all joy, my brothers, when you meet trials of various kinds, for you know that the testing of your faith produces steadfastness." While it is essential to understand that God did not design suffering to build character or endurance, trials can function as a 'refining fire' for our faith, clarifying what truly matters and driving us closer to God.

Anchoring Our Hope in God

Our ability to cope with suffering is directly correlated with where we place our hope. If our hope is in earthly success, relationships, or personal abilities, suffering will inevitably shake those foundations. But if our hope is anchored in God, we can find solace and courage, even amidst adversity. As the Psalmist wrote, "I have set the Lord always before me; because he is at my right hand, I shall not be shaken" (Psalm 16:8).

Pragmatic Steps: Applying Scriptural Principles

1. **Daily Devotion**: Consistent engagement with Scripture equips us with spiritual sustenance, making us resilient against the trials we may face (Psalm 119:105).

2. **Prayer**: An essential part of drawing near to God is consistent and heartfelt prayer (Philippians 4:6-7).

3. **Community Support**: The body of Christ is designed to provide encouragement and mutual upbuilding. There's value in leaning on trusted brothers and sisters in Christ during challenging times (Galatians 6:2).

4. **Acts of Service**: In moments of suffering, helping others can serve as a therapeutic act that shifts our focus from our own challenges and aligns us with Christ's example (Matthew 25:35-40).

5. **Professional Help**: It's okay to seek professional counseling and medical treatment as a complementary means of coping. Doing so is not a sign of spiritual weakness but can be a wise course of action (Proverbs 11:14).

Future Outlook: The Hope of Resurrection and a New World

Our earthly struggles are not the end of the story. The promise of resurrection and eternal life offers a profound sense of perspective. The existence of a new heaven and new earth, as described in Revelation 21, brings the assurance of a time when suffering, pain, and death will be no more. While we plan and live as though Jesus may return decades from now, the imperishable hope of eternal life should guide our choices and actions today.

The Journey Continues

The road ahead will undoubtedly contain more challenges, trials, and tests of faith. Yet, as we've seen, we have both a temporal guide in the form of God's Word and an eternal hope in the form of the Gospel promise.

God's will for us is not aimless wandering but purposeful living. By His grace, our relationship with Him can deepen, our character can grow more Christ-like, and our hope can become more firmly anchored in eternal truths. So, even as we face the sufferings and trials that this life inevitably brings, let us draw near to God, holding steadfastly to the promises in Scripture and buoyed by the hope of resurrection and eternal life.

Let us end this journey with the apostolic prayer for perseverance and hope from Romans 15:13, "May the God of hope fill you with all joy and peace in believing, so that by the power of the Holy Spirit you may abound in hope."

May we continue to draw near to God, seeking His wisdom, embracing His love, and living in the hope that, through Christ Jesus, better days—eternal days—are yet to come. Amen.

Building Resilience through Faith and Community

An Important Clarification

Firstly, it's crucial to articulate that while God didn't create suffering to foster growth, resilience, or character, He allows it. The existence of suffering serves as a poignant reminder of the inherent flaws in human independence from His sovereignty. Therefore, in the midst of suffering, it becomes all the more critical to turn to God and a supportive community of believers.

The Role of Faith in Building Resilience

Faith is not merely a set of intellectual assents or a collection of doctrines; it is a lived experience rooted in a relationship with God through Christ Jesus. When we face trials of any kind, whether emotional, physical, or spiritual, our faith becomes an anchor that holds us firm. Paul elucidates this beautifully in Romans 5:1-5. Even though the passage suggests that suffering produces character, it's vital to note that God didn't design suffering for this purpose; instead, suffering underscores the futility of life without God and implores us to turn to Him.

Trusting God's Sovereignty

When adversity strikes, one of the first questions we often ask is, "Why?" While it's human nature to seek understanding, it is faith that guides us to trust in God's sovereignty even when the answers are not apparent. Proverbs 3:5-6 advises us not to lean on our own understanding but to acknowledge God in all our ways. It is a submissive recognition that God is in control and has permitted certain situations for reasons we may never comprehend on this side of eternity.

Faith and Community: The Synergy of Resilience

The New Testament is filled with examples and exhortations about the value of community in the life of a believer. From the early church in Acts sharing all things in common, to the 'one another' commands scattered throughout the epistles, it's clear that faith was never intended to be a solo endeavor.

1. **Accountability**: A community of believers offers accountability. James 5:16 exhorts us to confess our sins to one another and pray for one another.

2. **Emotional and Spiritual Support**: The church provides a network of emotional and practical help in times of need (Acts 2:45; Galatians 6:2).

3. **Collective Worship and Prayer**: There's a unique strength and encouragement that comes from collective worship and prayer (Matthew 18:20).

4. **Wisdom from Elders**: Mature believers in the community can offer wisdom and biblical counsel, helping younger members navigate the challenges of life (Titus 2:2-5).

Practical Ways to Build Resilience through Faith and Community

1. **Regular Fellowship**: Consistently meeting with fellow believers provides an opportunity for mutual encouragement, prayer, and study of Scripture.

2. **Service**: Actively serving in church and community puts faith into action, enriches one's spiritual life, and provides a sense of purpose even in the midst of personal struggles.

3. **Discipleship and Mentorship**: Engaging in discipleship relationships helps fortify faith, provides accountability, and enhances resilience.

4. **Biblical Literacy**: The importance of continually diving into Scripture cannot be overstated. It equips us to discern God's will and fortifies us against trials.
5. **Prayer Groups**: Participating in or forming prayer groups offers a way to share burdens and joys and to intercede for each other.

Where To from Here?

While we navigate through the complexities of life, the object lesson of human existence continues to teach us. Let us build our resilience not on the fleeting philosophies of the world but on the unchangeable truths of Scripture and the mutual support of a God-centered community. As we do so, we must continually reflect on the transient nature of our current suffering in light of eternal promises. The temporal challenges should refine our focus on God, deepen our faith, and solidify the bonds within our spiritual community.

So, as you step forward into whatever challenges lie ahead, remember Paul's encouragement in 2 Corinthians 4:17-18: "For this light momentary affliction is preparing for us an eternal weight of glory beyond all comparison, as we look not to the things that are seen but to the things that are unseen."

May your faith be your anchor, and your community be your support, as you press forward into the life God has set before you. Amen.

Preparing for Future Trials: Equipping Ourselves Spiritually

The Reality of Future Trials

Scripture makes no attempt to shield us from the reality that trials are an inherent part of the human experience. In the book of James, it is not a question of "if" but "when" you face trials (James 1:2). As we prepare for the inevitable adversities that life will bring, we must recognize the need to be spiritually equipped. In a world rife with suffering, the Christian's ultimate strength comes from a spiritual foundation that is both unshakable and sustaining.

The Lesson of Suffering

While God didn't design suffering to foster growth, endurance, or character, it serves as an object lesson. This life serves as a lesson to demonstrate the inherent flaw in human independence from God's sovereignty. Suffering is a powerful reminder that we are not self-sufficient beings but rather, we are entirely dependent on God for our every need.

Equipping Ourselves with God's Word

The Apostle Paul refers to the Word of God as the "sword of the Spirit" in Ephesians 6:17. This metaphor implies that the Word is not only protective but also offensive against the spiritual forces that seek to disrupt our walk with God. The Scriptures serve multiple roles in our lives:

1. **Teaching**: The Word provides us with a foundational knowledge of who God is and what He requires of us (2 Timothy 3:16).

2. **Correction and Reproof**: Through Scripture, we receive the necessary correction and training to live righteously (2 Timothy 3:16).

3. **Wisdom and Discernment**: The Word equips us with the wisdom to navigate the complexities of life and discern between right and wrong (Hebrews 4:12).

Prayer as a Lifeline

Prayer is not simply a ritual but a direct line of communication with the Creator. It offers an opportunity for personal intimacy with God and provides a sense of peace and strength that can only come from Him (Philippians 4:6-7). Through prayer, we are spiritually rejuvenated, guided, and given the wisdom to face trials (James 1:5).

The Armor of God

Paul's vivid depiction of the "armor of God" in Ephesians 6:10-18 serves as an extended metaphor for the spiritual equipping we need. This armor includes:

1. **Truth**: Being honest and true in our dealings.
2. **Righteousness**: Living in a way that is pleasing to God.
3. **Gospel of Peace**: Being peacemakers and bearers of the good news.
4. **Faith**: Trusting God to do what He has promised.
5. **Salvation**: Maintaining our hope in Christ's saving grace.
6. **Word of God**: Constantly learning, meditating, and applying Scripture.

Community and Fellowship

While individual spiritual disciplines are critical, the New Testament emphasizes the importance of communal spiritual health. The church serves as a body of believers, each part indispensable and mutually dependent (1 Corinthians 12:12-27). The community serves to:

1. **Encourage**: Mutual support is vital for spiritual and emotional well-being (Hebrews 10:24-25).
2. **Teach**: Community provides a platform for collective learning and doctrinal stability (Colossians 3:16).
3. **Serve**: Through serving others, we embody Christ's love and message (Galatians 5:13).

Final Thoughts: Maintaining an Eternal Perspective

As we consider the trials that are to come, it is crucial to maintain an eternal perspective. This does not mean becoming so "heavenly minded" that we are of no "earthly good." Rather, it means balancing our immediate concerns with the lasting hope we have in Christ (Colossians 3:2).

Our lives are but a vapor, and our trials, however severe, are temporary. But God's promises are eternal. Though the nature of our trials may differ, their purpose remains the same: to teach us that apart from God, we can do nothing (John 15:5).

Equipping ourselves spiritually is not a one-time event but a lifelong process. It involves daily renewing our minds, constant prayer, regular engagement with God's Word, and active participation in a community of believers. These practices do not guarantee a life free from suffering; rather, they prepare us to face whatever comes with the unwavering hope and strength that can only come from a vibrant relationship with God.

So, let us move forward, fully equipped and spiritually prepared, as we continue to navigate the highs and lows of this earthly existence, keeping our eyes firmly fixed on the eternal promises that await us. Amen.

APPENDIX Other Related Books by Edward D. Andrews

LIFE DOES HAVE A PURPOSE: Discovering and Living Your Ultimate Purpose

ISBN-13: 979-8851221149

Christian Living: How to Succeed in the Christian Life

ISBN-13: 978-1945757136

FAITHFUL MINDS: A Biblical and Cognitive Behavioral Therapy Approach to Mental Health and Wellness

ISBN-13: 979-8378898909

UNSHAKABLE BELIEFS: Strategies for Strengthening and Defending Your Faith

ISBN-13: 979-8377383406

YOU CAN MAKE A DIFFERENCE: Why and How Your Christian Life Makes a Difference

ISBN-13: 978-1945757747

LET GOD USE YOU TO SOLVE YOUR PROBLEMS: GOD Will Instruct You and Teach You In the Way You Should Go

ISBN-13: 978-1945757860

THE POWER OF GOD: The Word That Will Change Your Life Today

ISBN-13: 978-1945757891

TURN OLD HABITS INTO NEW HABITS: Why and How the Bible Makes a Difference

ISBN-13: 978-1945757730

GOD WILL GET YOU THROUGH THIS: Hope and Help for Your Difficult Times

ISBN-13: 978-1945757723

MERE CHRISTIANITY REIMAGINED: Rediscovering the Faith for the 21st Century

ISBN-13: 979-8388787453

www.ingramcontent.com/pod-product-compliance
Lightning Source LLC
Chambersburg PA
CBHW070448050426
42451CB00015B/3388